ALSO BY BRUCE PANDOLFINI:

Let's Play Chess
Bobby Fischer's Outrageous Chess Moves
One-Move Chess by the Champions
Principles of the New Chess
The ABCs of Chess

KASPAROV'S WINNING CHESS TACTICS:

How He Thinks, How He Chooses

by BRUCE PANDOLFINI
NATIONAL MASTER

A FIRESIDE BOOK
Published by Simon & Schuster, Inc.
NEW YORK

For Roselyn, Sarah and Frances

A Fireside Book
Published by Simon & Schuster, Inc.
Simon & Schuster Building
Rockefeller Center
1230 Avenue of the Americas
New York, New York 10020
FIRESIDE and colophon are registered trademarks of
Simon & Schuster, Inc.
Designed by Stanley S. Drate/Folio Graphics Co. Inc.
Manufactured in the United States of America
10 9 8 7 6 5 4 3 2 1
Library of Congress cataloging in Publication Data
Pandolfini, Bruce.
    Kasparov's winning chess tactics.
    Includes 147 diagrammed positions taken from the
chess games of Gary Kasparov.
    "A Fireside book."
    Includes index.
    1. Kasparov, G. K. (Garri Kimovich)   2. Chess—
Collections of games.   3. Chess—Tournaments.
I. Kasparov, G. K. (Garri Kimovich)   II. Title.
III. Title: Winning chess tactics.
GV1439.K38P36   1986   794.1'59   86-17735
ISBN: 0-671-61985-3
ISBN 13: 978-0-671-61985-5

CONTENTS

ACKNOWLEDGMENTS

My thanks to Idelle Pandolfini for her industry, guidance and preparation of the manuscript; Bruce Alberston for his research and analysis; Carol Ann Caronia for her ideas and suggestions; Larry Tamarkin, Judy Shipman and Steve Immitt for producing the diagrams; and Deborah Bergman, Roane Carey and Nick Swyrydenko for their diligent editorial work.

INTRODUCTION

In the 1920s the leader of the hypermodern chess movement, the innovative Czechoslovakian grandmaster Richard Reti, was asked: "How many moves ahead do you see?"

Reti's reply, "As a rule, just one. The best," inspired the title of one of my books, *One-Move Chess by the Champions* (1985). Gary Kasparov, who gained the title shortly after that book's publication, was not included in it—he wasn't a champion at the time.

This book, *Kasparov's Winning Chess Tactics,* fetes the new title-holder, who at twenty-two is the youngest official chess champion ever. A vigorous, imaginative playing style, together with a forthright, congenial personality, have already made him the most dynamic figure in chess. What is his game, and how did it develop?

Kasparov's fundamental style is aggressive, centered on sharp tactics and grandly conceived attacks, an elaborate network of stratagems, shots, swindles, traps, pitfalls, schemes and threats to gain material or produce checkmate. It's a style that, in general, has brought Kasparov victory, though it involves tremendous risk.

Kasparov's Winning Chess Tactics consists of 147 diagrammed positions taken from the games and/or analysis of the new world champion and arranged in chronological chapters, from 1978 to 1985. Each example is clearly labeled and represented by a large diagram for easy use. Every position is discussed and described in chess notation to illustrate at least one instructive theme in its diagram.

Suppose, for example, you want to study pins (a common chess tactic defined in the glossary at the back of the book). You merely turn to the index in the back and find a listing of page numbers for positions where pins are critical. This approach is advised for anyone desiring to nail down specific tactics. Conversely, you can read the examples chronologically from the beginning regardless of theme. This approach approximates game conditions, which are almost always unpredictable. The setting for each example is given in the descriptive caption at the top of the page.

As you read through the explanations and commentary, you undoubtedly will be impressed with Kasparov's ability to calculate variations. The moves actually played are merely the tip of the iceberg. What happens under the surface of Kasparov's mind is staggering. His moves often reveal so little, they seem to make no sense. To understand them, you may have to penetrate the layers of analysis—as I do in these discussions—and try to enter his head.

Frequently, the same game has been used more than once to illustrate different tactics, a necessary and helpful method. In a few cases, a particular game offers situations in which either player might have won—perhaps Kasparov in one diagram and his opponent in the next. These juxtapositions clearly reveal the vicissitudes of top-level chess, where defeat is imminent for both contestants. In some instances, a position is so complicated that its analysis is unresolved and requires another diagram, which is given in the next position. Playing and reading through the first of such examples can help you understand the second.

Actual vs Possible

Two kinds of positions are shown: those that really occurred, designated as *Actual Position*, and those that might have occurred if either White or Black had chosen different moves from those actually played. Each of the latter is designated as *Possible Position*, followed by the hypothetical moves that inspired the tactic and the hypothetical result.

Many of the alternative possibilities appearing in the explanations come from Gary Kasparov's own notes as they appeared in Russian, Yugoslav, and other leading chess journals. These arcane symbols—together with my own—have been fleshed out and explained, often in detail, so that the reader can follow the logic of these moves, as if he were sitting with Gary Kasparov and discussing the game during the actual course of play.

Why This Book's Emphasis on Possible Moves?

I have included many Possible Positions because they are usually far more instructive than what actually transpired. They highlight interesting pitfalls that were averted by both players— those brilliant and valuable moves buried in the analysis, eluding ordinary observation. They tell us what would have happened if so-and-so had played such-and-such. Thus you can truly appreciate the meaning of the grandmaster's actual moves through study of the moves he avoided—the obvious isn't necessarily the best.

Basically, chess is a game of ideas. Actual moves, possible moves, analysis, strategy, tactics, threats, plans, whatever—all for the master are equal in the realm of thought and deserve equal time on their individual merits.

Masters tend to be more interested in the analysis of a game than in its actual moves, which may be incorrect or inexact. A move that is actually played is not necessarily superior to the alternative moves that were not, or to the reasoning guiding their selection. Many actual moves, in fact, are blunders, worthy of limited study. Nor does a victory mean that it was won with the best moves.

Analyzing alternative possibilities and their consequences brings us closer to the truth. Analysis may find a defense that would have saved the game for the loser. Comparing reasonable alternatives to the moves actually played uncovers the objectively best ideas.

Kasparov's Winning Chess Tactics is concerned with ideas. The emphasis is on the reasons for moves and their alternatives, and not on the actual moves themselves.

The Possible Positions were selected as in the following example, generated from a game Kasparov (White) and Lutikov (Black) played in the USSR in 1978.

The first eleven moves of the actual game were:

1.d4 Nf6 2. Nf3 d6 3. Nc3 Bg4 4. e4 Nbd7? 5. e5 Ng8 6. h3

Bxf3 7. Qxf3 c6 8. Bf4 d5 9. e6 fxe6 10. Bd3 Ngf6 11. Qe2 g6.
These moves lead to the following position:

Diagram A

Black's last move was **11 . . . g6,** which blocks the d3-h7 diagonal, guards against subsequent Queen checks at h5, and prepares to flank the Kingside Bishop. But before this move was played, it's likely that both grandmasters had to consider a very plausible variation beginning with a different 11th move for Black, 11 . . . Qb6 (diagram B), below:

Diagram B

Both players considered 11 . . . Qb6 as an alternative 11th move. Why? Because superficially it looks extremely promising. This maneuver of the Black Queen prepares Queenside castling while forking two of White's pawns, at d4 and b2. Black would consider this variation because he wants to win a pawn. Meanwhile White too examines it because he wants to retain the pawn.

After the possible continuation of 11 . . . Qb6 (diagram B), play might continue: 12. 0-0-0 0-0-0 13. Qxe6 Qxd4?

This is the Possible Position discussed in the scenario on page 22. Diagrams A and B, irrelevant to the problem there, are given here so that one can see how the Possible Positions in this book were developed from actual games. The above situation could have materialized if Black had played a different 11th move and then he and White had continued in this plausible two-move variation.

Considering alternative possibilities after the game is what superior players do as a matter of course. It reveals *how* and *why* specific moves were chosen. Focusing on the ideas of a great player rather than only on his moves gives greater insight into the game of chess.

Excepting an odd game or two from Kasparov's earlier career, those here presented are all taken from the highest tournament and match play. What they reveal is one of the great creative chess minds of the twentieth century. It is so easy to be floored by Kasparov's brilliance that we tend to forget he can lose an occasional game. It's only realistic to include some positions where Kasparov is on the wrong end of the roller coaster. Most of these are Possible Positions, where Kasparov is called upon to see through an ingenious trap, but in a few Kasparov actually loses. Yet, consider his opposition. It has included many outstanding players of the present—like Karpov, Spassky, and Petrosian—who were themselves world champions with an attained niche in goddess Caissa's hall of fame. Kasparov at twenty-two has chessed with peers and triumphed.

The real result of every game in the book, whether the position shown is actual or possible, is given in standard chess shorthand at the end of each analysis: 1–0 means White won; 0–1 means Black won. Some games ended in a draw. The number in parentheses indicates how many moves the game lasted. On pages 20–21, for example, Kasparov defeated Begun in 24 moves.

To illustrate how even great players can be beaten, a final section, "The Kasparov Test," includes ten traps set for Kasparov by his wily opponents. See how you fare against the same pitfalls. Do you avert them or are you snared? You may be surprised by the champion's own responses. He's human too.

This book can be used on several levels. First, it's a biography of a chess great through a collection of his masterpieces. Next, it's an instructional bible, classifying and arranging positions in categories. It is also a problem book in which you have to guess Kasparov's best moves. You will surely be entertained by his inventive genius. As Tarrasch commented: "Chess, like love, like music, has the power to make men happy." Enjoy yourself.

About Algebraic Notation

The best way to read this book is while sitting at a chessboard on the White side, with the pieces in their starting positions. Most of the material can be understood without playing out the moves, by either reading the descriptive comments or examining the helpful diagrams accompanying the text. But you will derive greater benefit if you learn the simplified algebraic notation offered here. The system works as follows:

- The board is regarded as an eight-by-eight graph with sixty-four squares in all.
- The *files* (the rows of squares going up the board) are lettered a through h, beginning from White's left.

- The *ranks* (the rows of squares going across the board) are numbered 1 through 8, beginning from White's nearest row.

You can therefore identify any square by combining a letter and a number, with the letter written first (see diagram C on page 14). For example, the square on which White's King stands in the original position is e1, while the original square for Black's King is e8. All squares are always named from White's point of view.

Symbols You Should Know
K means King
Q means Queen
R means Rook
B means Bishop
N means Knight

Pawns are not symbolized when recording the moves. But if referred to in discussions, they are named by the letter of the file occupied—the pawn on the b-file is the b-pawn. If a pawn makes a capture, one merely indicates the file the capturing pawn starts on. Thus, if a White pawn on b2 captures a Black pawn, Knight, Bishop, Rook, or Queen on a3, it is written **bxa3.** In indicating a capture, name the square captured, not the enemy unit.

x means captures
+ means check
0-0 means castles Kingside
0-0-0 means castles Queenside
! means good move
!! means very good move
? means questionable move
?? means blunder
1. means White's first move
1 . . . means Black's first move (when appearing independently of White's)
(1–0) means White wins
(0–1) means Black wins

Reading the Line Score of a Game

Consider diagram D. White could mate in three moves and it would be written this way:

   1. Nc7+ Kb8 2. Na6+ Ka8 3. Bc6 mate.

   1. Nc7+ means that White's first move was Knight moves to c7 giving check.

Kb8 means that Black's first move was King to b8.

   2. Na6+ means that White's second move was Knight to a6 check.

Ka8 means that Black's second move was King to a8.

   3. Bc6 mate means that White's third move was Bishop to c6 giving mate.

Note that the number of the move is written only once, appearing just before White's play. In this book, the actual moves are given in **boldface** type. The analyzed alternatives appear in regular type.

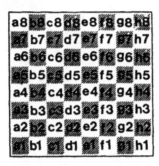

Diagram C

Diagram D

KASPAROV'S WINNING CHESS TACTICS:

How He Thinks, How He Chooses

1

EARLY YEARS

Garik Kimovich Wainstein was born April 13, 1963, in Baku, the capital city of Azerbaidzhan. With a population of one million, Baku lies on the east-central shore of the Caspian Sea. Its mild temperatures make Baku something of a resort area as well as a Soviet oil refining center. When Gary was nine his father, Kim Moiseyevich Wainstein, died, and Gary and his mother, Krla Kasparian, went to live with her parents, also residents of Baku. Upon reaching the legal age of twelve it was quite natural that his surname should be changed to that of his maternal grandparents (Kasparov is merely the Russian version of the Armenian Kasparian).

There is an unverified story that tells how six-year-old Gary, without having yet learned the moves, solved a chess puzzle from the local newspaper column. This story is not hard to believe. In any event when Gary was seven, a neighboring lad, Rostik Korunsky, took Gary to the chess club at the Young Pioneers, a national Soviet youth organization. There Gary caught the watchful interest of chess trainer Oleg Privorotsky, who still remembers him quite well. Privorotsky was particularly impressed by Gary's seemingly photographic memory, as he learned raw statistical data, world championship game moves and results by heart. And there was total concentration as Gary tried to unravel the complexities of a position. Naturally, the beauty of a combinational finish made a lasting impression on him, as did the dynamic games of the late world champion, Alexander Alekhine.

Quite rapidly, Gary hit all the right rungs on the ladder without missing a step. In June of 1973, Gary, age ten, participated in the Youth Team Championship at Vilnius. Gary managed to finish without a loss against much older boys and his prowess attracted the attention of two trainers, Alexander Shakharov and Alexander Nikitin. Both were associated with the exclusive Botvinnik school and, only one month after Vilnius, Gary was invited to attend a session at the school.

Mikhail Botvinnik, a former world champion (1948-57, 1958-60, 1961-63) and a chess immortal, ran his school in unusual style. The courses were conducted primarily by correspondence, but two or three times a year, usually during school vacations, the students had the chance to meet with their teacher. At these sessions a student was given a tough assignment specifically geared to his needs. This independent work, Botvinnik felt, was the key to developing a talent to the fullest.

Gary remained with the school for five years (1973-78), and Botvinnik recounts how during the February 1978 session, in need of a helper, he asked Gary to be his assistant, for "in the opening and sometimes in analysis" Kasparov could "outdo anyone." Gary, for his part, mastered indestructible basics. About Botvinnik's school Kasparov has said, "There is no price I could name for the things I got from the course during the next five years. He does not . . . impose his view on his pupils."

The knowledge Kasparov acquired at the Botvinnik school soon yielded some surprisingly good results. At age twelve he won the 1976 USSR Junior Championship at Tbilisi. The following January at Riga he duplicated the feat. A few years later, a rapid succession of events found Gary playing in the World Cadet Championships in France. At these 1976 and 1977 matches he distinguished himself but he was still raw in experience. Still his performances were undeniably good. The breakthrough into senior chess occurred in January of 1978 when Gary was fourteen. Though not yet a master and without international rating, he was allowed to play in the 8th Sokolsky Memorial Tournament at Minsk. And play he did! By taking the first prize Gary also gained the honored title "Soviet Master of Sport." In that tournament, moreover, Gary collected his first grandmaster scalp, that of A. Lutikov. Minsk was a memorable tournament and a great step forward.

Six months later, Kasparov won equal first at Daugaplis, a thirteen-round qualifying event for the Soviet championship. Catching fire in rounds two through eight, Gary scored five-and-a-half out of six and never looked back. He was just fifteen. Gary's co-winner at Daugaplis, who lost out on tie breaks, was none other than Igor Ivanov. Several years later Igor decided to seek his fortunes in the West, where he became known in the U.S.A. as the man who swept home all the Grand Prix Prizes.

The 46th USSR Championship, held in Tbilisi in December 1978, was an awesome test for young Kasparov. In a field of no less than sixteen grandmasters, Gary had to set realistic goals. First was too much to hope for, but the top nine would automatically be entered into next year's championship, avoiding all the qualifying procedures. Gary placed ninth exactly, with four wins, four losses and nine draws. A good showing for anyone making a first appearance in a Soviet championship.

WHITE: **Kasparov**   TACTIC: **MATING ATTACK**
BLACK: **Begun**
WHERE: **USSR 1978**
ACTUAL POSITION

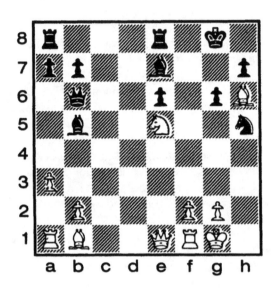

WHITE TO MOVE

ANALYSIS: Here Kasparov is down a pawn and his Rook at f1 is threatened by Black's light-square Bishop. But White's pieces are bearing on the Black Kingside, where there are plenty of holes and loose ends. Kasparov penetrates Black's flimsy front with the breakthrough sacrifice **1. Bxg6!**, shattering his opponent's Kingside. If Black counters with 1 . . . Bxf1, then White simply gobbles the Black Knight (2. Bxh5) and continues to threaten to capture at f1 and e8. In fact if Black is not careful in this line, he can even get mated. After 2. Bxh5, for example, retreating the Bishop to b5 loses to 3. Bf7 + Kh8 4. Ng6 + hxg6 5. Qe5 +, when mate on g7 ensues in two moves.

The most direct response to **1. Bxg6!**, taking the audacious Bishop with 1 . . . hxg6, also fails after 2. Qe4 Bf8 (trying to create a Knight and Bishop block on g7), when White wraps up matters anyway with 3. Qxg6+ Ng7 (saving the Knight) 4. Ng4. Black would then have to surrender his Queen to stop 5. Nf6+ and 6. Qh7 mate.

In the actual game, Black withdrew his Knight **1 . . . Nf6** and was compelled to resign after another Bishop sacrifice, **2. Bxh7+!**. If Black had continued 2 . . . Kxh7, then 3. Qb1+, followed by a Queen invasion on g6, is decisive. After 3 . . . Kh8 4. Qg6, for example, White threatens mate by both Qg7 and Nf7. Taking the Bishop with the Knight 2 . . . Nxh7 also loses, for 3. Qe4 prepares a shift to g6 with looming catastrophe (note that 3 . . . Nf8 is answered by 4. Qg4+). **Black Resigned.**
1–0 (24)

WHITE: **Kasparov**   TACTIC: **MATING NET**
BLACK: **Lutikov**
WHERE: **USSR 1978**
POSSIBLE POSITION

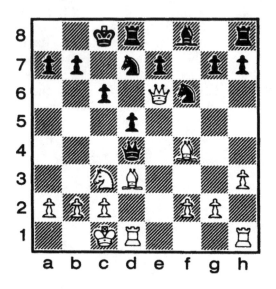

WHITE TO MOVE

ANALYSIS: White pulls an old and familiar swindle. It begins with **1. Qxc6 +**. After the forced **1 . . . bxc6**, it concludes with **2. Ba6**, a criss-cross mate. Some people call this Boden's Mate, after a 19th century British master. Whatever the name, it "bodens" unwell for Black. **White Wins.**
1–0 (53)

WHITE: Mihaljchisin
BLACK: Kasparov
WHERE: USSR 1978
POSSIBLE POSITION

TACTIC: DISCOVERED ATTACK,
FORK, TRAP

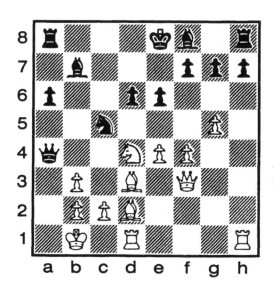

BLACK TO MOVE

ANALYSIS: Black's Queen is attacked, though apparently he can take White's hanging Knight at d4. Kasparov's opponent thought not, and perhaps believed he was on the verge of a Queen trap. After **1 . . . Qxd4 2. Bc3** the Queen indeed seems trapped. But **2 . . . Nxe4 3. Bxd4 Nc3 +** regains the Queen the next move with **4 . . . Bxf3** while forking the two Rooks. End result, Black garners the exchange. **Black Wins.**
1–0 (82)

WHITE: **Kasparov**   TACTIC: **MATING ATTACK**
BLACK: **Panchenko**
WHERE: **USSR 1978**
POSSIBLE POSITION

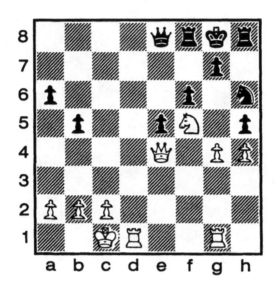

WHITE TO MOVE

ANALYSIS: Black hopes to extricate his King and reach the endgame a pawn up. In the following line, he's doomed in the middlegame: **1. Nxg7** (ripping up the Black King's position) **1 . . . Kxg7 2. gxh5+ Kf7 3. Qb7+ Ke6** (3 . . . Qe7 loses the Queen to 4. Rd7 or 4. Rg7+) **4. Qd5+ Ke7** (4 . . . Kf5 allows 5. Rdf1 mate) **5. Rg7+** and mate next move. **White Wins.**
1–0 (35)

WHITE: Kasparov   TACTIC: **MATING ATTACK**
BLACK: Palatnik
WHERE: USSR 1978
POSSIBLE POSITION

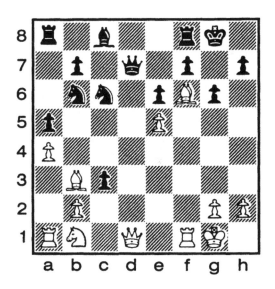

WHITE TO MOVE

ANALYSIS: Rather than trade Queens, White opts for mate: **1. Qc1!** (threatening 2. Qh6 and 3. Qg7 mate). Black can only avert this disaster by heavy losses. For example: 1 . . . Qd4 + 2. Kh1 Nd7 3. Qh6 Nxf6 4. exf6 Qxf6 5. Rxf6. **White Wins.** 1–0 (37)

2

SWEET SIXTEEN

On his sixteenth birthday, April 13, 1979, the Yugoslav Banja Luka tournament got under way. The only non-FIDE-rated player in the field of sixteen (fourteen were grandmasters), Gary broke from the pack with eleven-and-a-half points out of a possible fifteen.

In second place, two full points behind, was the Swede Ulf Andersson, while former world champion Tigran Petrosian was two-and-a-half points behind. Gary easily achieved the first norm for a grandmaster (ten-and-a-half points) and stunned the chess world with his dazzling entrance onto the international stage.

In November and December Kasparov was in Minsk for the 47th USSR Championship. Based on his Soviet rating of 2510, he was expected to score only seven-and-a-half points in the eighteen-man round robin. But for Gary a score of seven-and-a-half points was a thing of the past. Obviously, he was still improving and his rating, lagging behind, could not reflect his real power. His actual score, ten points and a share of third place, more accurately estimated his developing strength.

WHITE: **Kasparov**   TACTIC: **MATING ATTACK**
BLACK: **Browne**
WHERE: **Banja Luka 1979**
ACTUAL POSITION

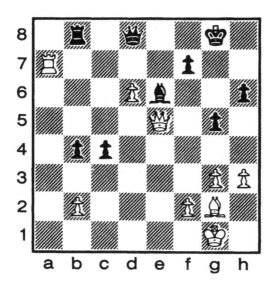

WHITE TO MOVE

ANALYSIS: With a Rook on the 7th rank, a dangerous passed pawn, and a commanding post for his Queen, White holds the key cards. The winning play was **1. Be4!**. Not perceiving White's scheme, Browne continued **1 . . . c3** and gave up after **2. Bh7+ Kxh7** (2 . . . Kf8 3. Qh8 mate) **3. Qxe6.** There's no satisfactory defense to the threat of 4. Rxf7+. **White Won.**
1–0 (39)

WHITE: **Sibarevic**   TACTIC: **DISCOVERED ATTACK**
BLACK: **Kasparov**
WHERE: **Banja Luka 1979**
ACTUAL POSITION

BLACK TO MOVE

ANALYSIS: Black plays **1 . . . Qxe2**, foisting the double threat 2 . . . Bxg2+ (winning White's Queen by discovery) and 2 . . . Qxg2 mate. White can cope with both by 2. Qg3, but that leaves the Bishop at c5 floating to the Rook. And 2. Rg1 loses the Queen to 2 . . . Bxg2+ . In a futile position, **White Resigned.** 0–1 (32)

WHITE: **Kasparov**   TACTIC: **CORRIDOR MATE**
BLACK: **Polugaevsky**
WHERE: **USSR 1979**
ACTUAL POSITION

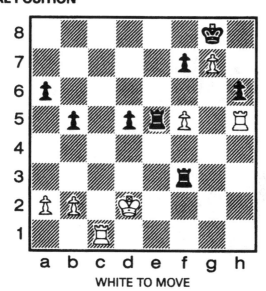

WHITE TO MOVE

ANALYSIS: If White checks on the back rank he loses his g-pawn, nor does he want to unnecessarily tie down a Rook to the pawn's defense. The time-gaining solution is **1. f6!**, based on four objectives:

A) To protect the g-pawn.

B) To expose an attack to the Rook at e5 from the Rook at h5.

C) To project 2. Rc8 + .

D) To prepare the capture of Black's h-pawn, planning a subsequent Rh8 + .

With two corridor mates waiting for him (at c8 or shortly at h8), Polugaevsky's only hope is to keep checking. What's fascinating here is Kasparov's ability to elude this checking sequence without abating his own threats. Thus **1 . . . Rf2+ 2. Kd3 Rf3+ 3. Kd4 Re4+ 4. Kxd5 Re8.** For a moment, the checks take time out and Black must stop White's Rc8+. But after **5. Rxh6**, the checks renew: **5 . . . Rf5+ 6. Kd4!** (6. Kd6? Re6+ is followed by 7 . . . Rxf6) **6 . . . Rf4+ 7. Kc5 Re5+ 8. Kb6 Re6+ 9. Rc6. Black Resigned.**

1–0 (37)

WHITE: **Veingold**   TACTIC: **KNIGHT FORK**
BLACK: **Kasparov**
WHERE: **USSR 1979**
POSSIBLE POSITION

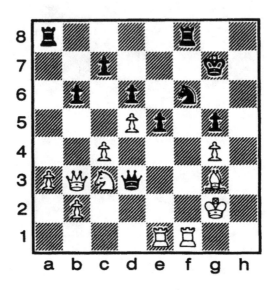

BLACK TO MOVE

ANALYSIS: This line was suggested by Kasparov in a published analysis. Black regains the sacrificed material with **1 . . . Ne4!**. If **2. Bh2** (or 2. Bf2 Rxf2+ 3. Rxf2 Qg3+ with mate next), **2 . . . Rxf1 3. Rxf1 Qxf1+! 4. Kxf1 Nd2+**, followed by **5. Nxb3. Black Wins.** Kasparov's overall board sense and multiplex vision have no equal in contemporary chess.
1–0 (41)

WHITE: **Kasparov**   TACTIC: **DISCOVERED ATTACK**
BLACK: **Yusupov**
WHERE: **USSR 1979**
POSSIBLE POSITION

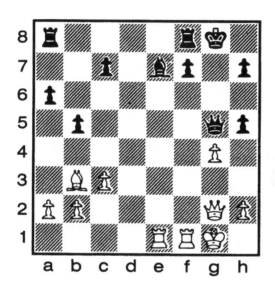

WHITE TO MOVE

ANALYSIS: In this imaginary variation, Black has just played his Queen from e5 to g5, so that it's tied to the defense of the Bishop at e7. Also his Kingside is somewhat exposed, as illustrated by **1. Rf5.** If 1 . . . Qh4 (keeping his eye on the untended Bishop), then 2. Re4 and there is no adequate parry to the coming 3. gxh5, which at that point wins the Queen. Note that the immediate 2. Rxh5 hangs the Rook at e1. **White Wins.**
1–0 (41)

WHITE: **Kasparov**   TACTIC: **OUTSIDE PASSED PAWN**
BLACK: **Yusupov**
WHERE: **USSR 1979**
ACTUAL POSITION

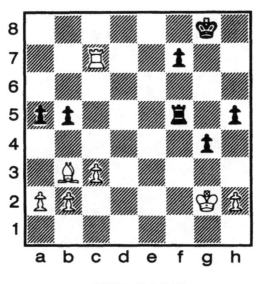

WHITE TO MOVE

ANALYSIS: Ahead by a Bishop for a pawn, Kasparov elected to exchange his material advantage for an easily won King-and-pawn endgame. He played **1. Rxf7!**. To quote Nimzovich's *Chess Praxis:* "White unhesitatingly gives back the whole of his material gain . . . That is how it should be done. Do not always hold on blindly to your gains. To play with freedom (turn one advantage into another), that is the watchword." No disputing that.

Play concluded: **1 . . . Rxf7 2. Kg3** (of course White needn't take the pinned Rook pronto, so he gains a tempo) **2 . . . a4 3. Bxf7+ Kxf7 4. Kh4 Kg6 5. b3** (preparing to create a passed c-pawn) **5 . . . a3 6. c4 bxc4 7. bxc4** (the outside passed pawn) **7 . . . Kf5 8. Kxh5 Ke4 9. Kxg4 Kd4 10. h4,** and **Black Resigned.**
1–0 (41)

WHITE: **Sveshnikov**　　　　TACTIC: **PENETRATION**
BLACK: **Kasparov**
WHERE: **USSR 1979**
ACTUAL POSITION

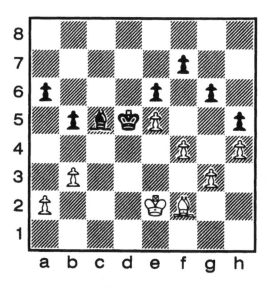

WHITE TO MOVE

ANALYSIS: Black's centralized King and Bishop are geared for attack, but can they actually nip into White's camp? After **1. Bxc5?**, Kasparov does just that: **1 . . . Kxc5 2. Kd3 Kb4 3. Kc2 Ka3 4. Kb1 a5 5. Ka1 a4 6. bxa4 Kxa4** (it's only a draw after 6 . . . bxa4 7. Kb1 Kb4 8. Kb2) **7. Kb1** (7. Kb2 b4 leads to the same position as in the actual game) **7 . . . Ka3 8. Ka1 b4 9. Kb1 b3,** and **White Resigned**. The King marches along the third rank and collects the g-pawn after 10. axb3 Kxb3. **Black Won.**

But there was really a draw here. Instead of **1. Bxc5?**, White should have refused the trade with 1. Be1. Black is out in the cold after 1 . . . b4 2. Kf3!, when 2 . . . Kd4 is answered by 3. Bf2 +. Surprisingly, centering White's King by 2. Kd3? (instead of Kf3) actually loses after 2 . . . a5 3. Ke2 Ke4 4. Bd2 Bd4 5. Bc1 Bc3 6. Be3 Be1!, when Black squeezes in.
0–1 (43)

AT THE FOOT OF MOUNT OLYMPUS

There was no time to rest. In January the ten-player Soviet Team was off to Skara, Sweden, for the European Team Championship. Kasparov as second reserve scored five-and-a-half out of six, a 91.6 percentage, and best on the Soviet team. Only two months later the USSR Central Chess Club organized an international tournament in Baku. Playing at home, Gary scored an impressive eleven-and-a-half out of fifteen, carting off first prize. With this Gary also gained his second norm for the title of International Grandmaster, and, once again, he overfulfilled the requirement.

In August, off to Dortmund, West Germany, as the Soviet representative for the World Junior Championship, Gary was already sporting a FIDE rating of 2595. This, coupled with victories in senior tournaments, made him the clear favorite, and his score of ten-and-a-half points out of a possible thirteen easily outdistanced England's prodigy, Nigel Short, who settled for second place with nine points.

Came November and Kasparov was a hundred miles off the Southern coast of Sicily, on the island of Malta. There the International Chess Federation staged its biennial Chess Olympics, involving matches of four-man teams (two reserves are permitted). From their inception (Helsinki 1952), these Olympics had been won by the Soviet team every time they played until the Buenos Aires Tournament in 1978, when the Hungarian team scored a stunning upset. The Hungarians were also expected to be a forceful team at Malta, which they were. The Soviets were only able to edge them out by the narrowest margin of tie breaks. And it was generally agreed that both teams had displayed equally high levels of chess play. Without Kasparov's fine score as second reserve (79 percent) not even tie breaks would have held off the Hungarians.

WHITE: **Kasparov**   TACTIC: **PIN**
BLACK: **Kuijpers**
WHERE: **DORTMUND** 1980
ACTUAL POSITION

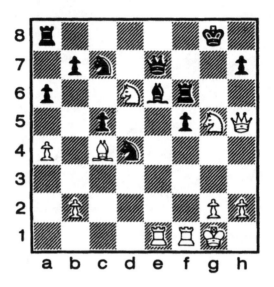

WHITE TO MOVE

ANALYSIS: The a2-g8 diagonal gives the right slant. With two Bishops on it along with the Black King, who can doubt a pinning bloodbath? Kasparov whirled to instantaneous victory with **1. Nxf5! Nxf5 2. Nxe6 Nxe6 3. Rxe6 Rxe6 4. Qxf5 Re8 5. Re1,** for Black must lose at least a piece. **Black Resigned.**
1–0 (28)

WHITE: Kasparov TACTIC: DISCOVERED ATTACK
BLACK: Kuijpers
WHERE: Dortmund 1980
POSSIBLE POSITION

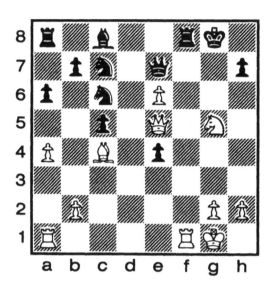

WHITE TO MOVE

ANALYSIS: Yes, Black does have an extra Knight, but White is one up with a fantastic conception. The raw material is the Queen, Bishop, Knight and a potential passed pawn monster. Incisively, White plays **1. Qxc7!!** (so that after 1 . . . Qxc7, White can erupt a volcanic discovered check by 2. e7). Black interjected **1 . . . Rxf1 + 2. Rxf1** before capturing **2 . . . Qxc7**, but that fades away to **3. e7 + Be6** (to clear the back rank) **4. Rf8 +**. If **4 . . . Rxf8,** then **5. exf8/Q + Kxf8 6. Nxe6 +** forks the King and Queen, and White is up a piece. **White Wins.**
1–0 (28)

WHITE: Arnason   TACTIC: **MATING NET**
BLACK: Kasparov
WHERE: Dortmund 1980

ACTUAL POSITION

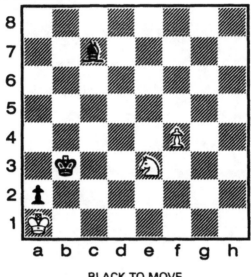

BLACK TO MOVE

ANALYSIS: Black could be tempted to take the f-pawn with his Bishop and then disturb with a check along the a1-h8 diagonal. But logically, that goes nowhere after 1 . . . Bxf4 2. Nc4!!, when Black can't take the Knight without dropping his a-pawn, which is necessary to fashion a win. Meanwhile, from c4, the Knight banners a series of irritating checks ·at d2 (or a5) and c4. For example, after 1 . . . Bxf4 2. Nc4, Black could try 2 . . . Bc1, but 3. Nd2+ Ka3 (or 3 . . . Bxd2 stalemate) 4. Nc4+ perpetuates the draw.

    Kasparov instead found the powerful **1 . . . Ba5**, intending 2 . . . Bc3 mate. White then played **2. Nd5**, and capitulated after **2 . . . Bd2**, unable to grapple with the impending 3 . . . Bc1 and 4 . . . Bb2 mate. **White Resigned.**
0–1 (58)

WHITE: Kasparov   TACTIC: PIN
BLACK: Hjorth
WHERE: Dortmund 1980
ACTUAL POSITION

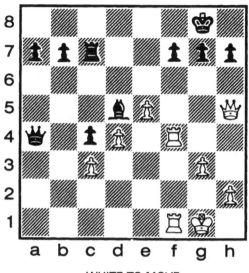

WHITE TO MOVE

ANALYSIS: White's exchange-up position is almost neutralized by Black's extra pawn and Queenside possibilities. Meanwhile, Black's Bishop and Rook protect the Achilles heel, f7. Kasparov bypassed the issue with **1. e6!**, when 1 . . . fxe6 welcomes 2. Rf8 mate. So Black continued **1 . . . Bxe6** and incurred **2. d5**, which is designed to dissuade the Bishop from the f-pawn. Black pinned the d-pawn to White's Queen, **2 . . . Qb5** (2 . . . Rc5 3. Rxf7! wins, while 2 . . . g6 3. Qh4 bottles Black up). Engaging here is 3. Qe5, and if Black blunders with 3 . . . Rc5?, White plays 4. Qxe6!. But the simple 3 . . . Rc8 (instead of 3 . . . Rc5?) suffices to keep the ship afloat. White doesn't get far either with 3. Qh4 (threatening 4. Qd8+) 3 . . . Qxd5 4. Rd4 g5!.

A much stronger continuation is Kasparov's actual move, **3. Rh4!! Qc5+ 4. Rf2 Bxd5** (or 4 . . . Qxd5 5. Qxh7+ Kf8 6. Rd4!, when moving Black's Queen to safety permits 7. Qh8+ Ke7 8. Qd8 mate) **5. Rd4! Rd7 6. Rf5** and the Bishop goes. **Black Resigned.**
1–0 (27)

WHITE: **Kasparov**
BLACK: **Speelman**
WHERE: **Malta 1980**
ACTUAL POSITION

TACTIC: **TRAPPED PIECE**

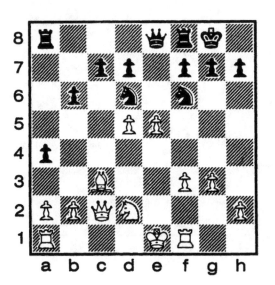

WHITE TO MOVE

ANALYSIS: Speelman has faced a hard day from the very open-ing stages, and it's clear that once White's King leaves the e-file Black loses a Knight. Nevertheless, White knows that just any-thing won't work. Kasparov demonstrates both care and accu-racy: **1. Kf2** (exiting the e-file and preparing to castle by hand) **1 ...Nxd5 2. Qd3!** (but not 2. exd6, for 2 . . . Ne3 gives Black a fork on the Queen and Rook) **2 . . . Qe6**. Here, Black accepts the loss of his Knight in order to activate his Queen. If instead 2 . . . Nxc3, White captures the Knight on d6 with his pawn and the Knight on c3 is trapped anyway. In the game, Kasparov played **3. exd6** and duly converted his advantage to a win. **White Won.**
1–0 (37)

WHITE: **Kasparov**
BLACK: **Marjanovic**
WHERE: **Malta 1980**

TACTIC: **MATING ATTACK**

ACTUAL POSITION

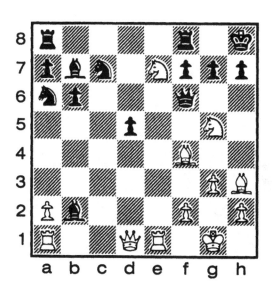

WHITE TO MOVE

ANALYSIS: White has four minor pieces posted on the Kingside, while Black's counterparts are all on the opposite wing. That, plus White's Queen about to bow in on h5, makes the difference. But first, the opening zinger: **1. Nxh7!**. Now if 1 . . . Kxh7, then 2. Qh5+ wins Black's Queen (2 . . . Qh6 3. Bxh6). Black stings back **1 . . . Qd4**, leading to **2. Qh5 g6 3. Qh4 Bxa1** (finally, but there's nothing better anyway) **4. Nf6+ Black Resigned**, for 4 . . . Kg7 5. Nf5+! gxf5 6. Qh6 is mate.
1–0 (23)

WHITE: Kasparov   TACTIC: DISCOVERED ATTACK
BLACK: Ligterink
WHERE: Malta 1980
ACTUAL POSITION

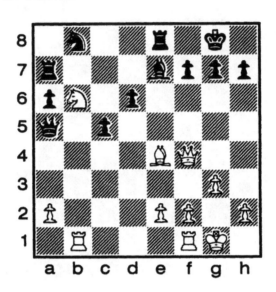

WHITE TO MOVE

ANALYSIS: It's clear that Black's pieces are unstrung as a team, and that bodes ill when facing a fiendish attacker like Gary Kasparov. After **1. Nc8!!**, Black had to choose among several unpleasant continuations:

A) If he takes the Knight, 1 . . . Rxc8, then 2. Qf5! forks the Rook and threatens to invade at h7.

B) If he moves his hounded Rook to safety, 1 . . . Rc7, then 2. Rxb8 Bf8 (to maintain the pin) 3. Nxd6! (unpin) 3 . . . Rxb8 4. Nc4! (deflecting the guard) and a Rook must fall.

C) What he actually played was **1 . . . Nc6**, which dissipated into **2. Nxa7 Nxa7 3. Bd5**, threatening the f-pawn as well as Rb7. **Black Resigned.**
1–0 (24)

WHITE: Renman   TACTIC: **CENTRALIZATION**
BLACK: Kasparov
WHERE: Skara 1980
ACTUAL POSITION

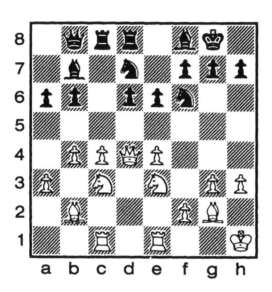

BLACK TO MOVE

ANALYSIS: In such a position Kasparov is able to play **1 ... Nc5!**, when the only satisfactory response to the Knight fork at b3 is **2. Rc2.** On 2. bxc5 instead, Black scoops up the Queen with 2 ... dxc5, for she's without a safe retreat. After **2 ... e5** forcing **3. Qd1**, Black appropriates a good center pawn with **3 ... Ncxe4. Black won.**
0–1 (45)

WHITE: **Renman**
BLACK: **Kasparov**
WHERE: **Skara 1980**
ACTUAL POSITION

TACTIC: **MATING ATTACK**

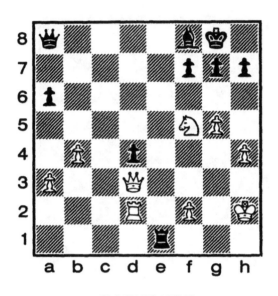

BLACK TO MOVE

ANALYSIS: Kasparov scored with **1 . . . Qh1 + 2. Kg3 g6!**. **White Resigned.** Possible continuations were:

A) 3. Nxd4 Bd6 + 4. f4 Rg1 + 5. Kf2 Qh2 + 6. Ke3 Qxf4 + 7. Ke2 Qf1 + 8. Ke3 Rg3 +, knocking off the Queen.

B) 3. Nh6 + Bxh6 4. gxh6 Rg1 + 5. Kf4 Qxh4 + 6. Ke5 Rg5 + 7. Kd6 Qf4 + 8. Kc6 (a lengthy King trek) 8 . . . Qf6 + simply winning. 0–1 (45)

WHITE: Spiridonov TACTIC: **REMOVING THE GUARD,**
BLACK: Kasparov   **KNIGHT FORK**
WHERE: Skara 1980
POSSIBLE POSITION

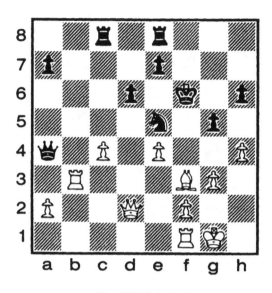

BLACK TO MOVE

ANALYSIS: For now White's Bishop depends on the defending Rook at b3. If the Rook should be captured, so would the Bishop, so would the Queen. Black continues here **1 . . . Qxb3** (removing the guard), and if **2. axb3**, then **2 . . . Nxf3+** followed by the mopping up **3 . . . Nxd2. Black Wins.**
0–1 (40)

WHITE: Spiridonov   TACTIC: PIN
BLACK: Kasparov
WHERE: Skara 1980

ACTUAL POSITION

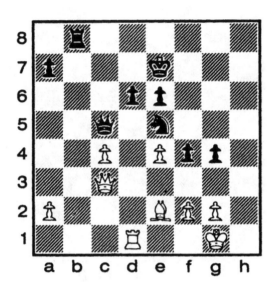

BLACK TO MOVE

ANALYSIS: White can get knotted up here pretty quickly. The roping starts after **1 . . . g3 2. Rf1 gxf2+ 3. Rxf2 Rb1+ 4. Bf1 Qe3! 5. Qxe3** (5. Qa5 Rb2 6. Qc7+ Nd7 is conclusive) **5 . . . fxe3 6. Rc2 Nxc4!**, when, rather than hang by his thumbs, **White Resigned.** If 7. Rxc4 (else 7 . . . Nd2), then 7 . . . e2 concludes. 0–1 (40)

WHITE: **Kasparov**   TACTIC: **SMOTHERED MATE**
BLACK: **Pribly**
WHERE: **Skara 1980**
POSSIBLE POSITION

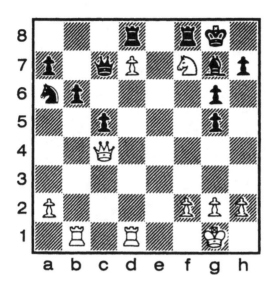

WHITE TO MOVE

ANALYSIS: Black should have captured the Knight with his Rook on the previous move, instead of allowing this debacle by moving his King into a potential double check. White now swivels out the great crowd pleaser, the smothered mate popularized by Philidor's analysis from the 18th century (though it actually predates that period considerably). The game concludes: **1. Nh6+ + Kh8 2. Qg8+ Rxg8 3. Nf7 mate. White Wins.**
1–0 (31)

WHITE: **Kasparov**
BLACK: **Pribly**
WHERE: **Skara 1980**
POSSIBLE POSITION

TACTIC: **MATING ATTACK**

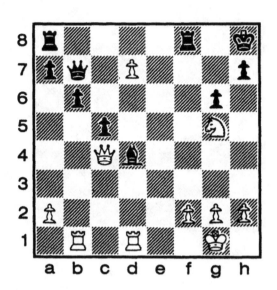

WHITE TO MOVE

ANALYSIS: Black has just played his Bishop to block the Rook that supports the d-pawn. It's a weak defensive measure that fizzles down before our very eyes. White demolishes it with **1. Rxd4 cxd4 2. Qxd4+** After **2 . . . Kg8 3. Ne6** the win is forced:

A) 3 . . . Rf7 4. d8/Q+, when 4 . . . Rxd8 leads to 5. Qxd8+ Rf8 6. Qxf8 mate.

B) 3 . . . Kf7 4. Re1 Rg8 (to guard g7) 5. Ng5+ Kf8 6. Qf6 mate. **White Wins.**

1–0 (31)

WHITE: **Kasparov**   TACTIC: PIN
BLACK: **Pribly**
WHERE: **Skara 1980**
POSSIBLE POSITION

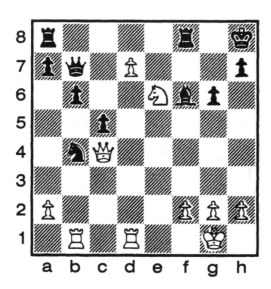

WHITE TO MOVE

ANALYSIS: White commences with a pin, **1. Qf4!**. If **1 . . . Nc6** (1
. . . Nd5 permits 2. Qd6!, which is very juicy), then **2. Nxf8** is the
right time to take the Rook. After **2 . . . Rxf8 3. d8/Q! Nxd8 4.
Rxd8**, White assumes the catbird seat with an exchange to the
good. If 4 . . . Bxd8, then 5. Qxf8 is mate. And if 4 . . . Rxd8, then
5. Qxf6 + wipes up the floor. **White Wins.**
1–0 (31)

WHITE: **Kasparov**
BLACK: **Pribly**
WHERE: **Skara 1980**
POSSIBLE POSITION

TACTIC: **PIN**

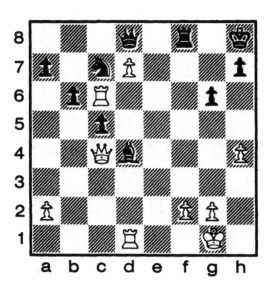

WHITE TO MOVE

ANALYSIS: How many times is Black's Knight attacked? Once? Look again, especially after **1. Rxd4! cxd4 2. Qxd4+ Kg8 3. Qc4+**. After Black gets out of check, White plays 4. Rxc7, winning the Knight with a dominating position. **White Wins.**
1–0 (31)

WHITE: **Kasparov**   TACTIC: **PASSED PAWN**
BLACK: **Pribly**
WHERE: **Skara 1980**
POSSIBLE POSITION

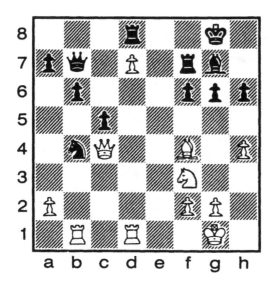

WHITE TO MOVE

ANALYSIS: White has an eager d-pawn, which is blockaded by a Black Rook and is under fire. The piercing of the blockade is similar to a famous early-career position of Fischer's. White begins by sacking the exchange with **1. Rxb4 cxb4.** That opens the c-file, allowing **2. Bc7,** where the Bishop is protected by the Queen and the Queen pins the Rook at f7. Black tries **2 . . . b5,** to either force the Queen from the defense of the Bishop or off the pinning diagonal. This frees the Rook to participate in a capture of the troublesome d-pawn. But White can get two Rooks for the Queen immediately and insure his pawn's subsequent advance with **3. Qxf7+ Kxf7 4. Bxd8.** The irrepressible pawn then Queens by force (if 4 . . . f5, then 5. Be7). **White Wins.**
1–0 (31)

WHITE: **Kasparov**
BLACK: **Csom**
WHERE: **Baku 1980**
ACTUAL POSITION

TACTIC: **MATING ATTACK**

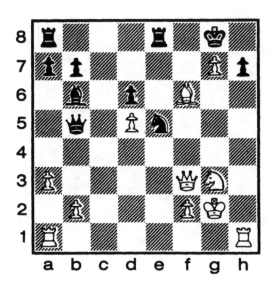

WHITE TO MOVE

ANALYSIS: The elements of a mating attack were patently here. A wedged-in pawn at g7, a supporting Bishop, an open h-file, and a mobilized Queen and Knight. The river flowed freely all the way to mate: **1. Nf5!** (threatening 2. Nh6 mate) **1 . . . Nf7 2. Rxh7!** and **Black Resigned**. Kasparov's favorite blasting cap—the Rook—did what it was hired for. The concluding moves might have been 2 . . . Kxh7 3. Qh5+ Kg8 4. Qh8+ Nxh8 5. gxh8/Q+ Kf7 6. Qg7 mate.
1–0 (29)

WHITE: Kasparov   TACTIC: CENTRALIZATION
BLACK: Martinovic
WHERE: Baku 1980
ACTUAL POSITION

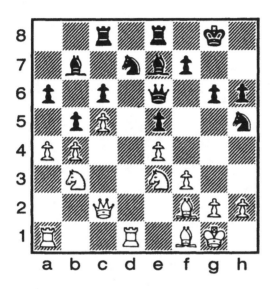

WHITE TO MOVE

ANALYSIS: It's cramped-up time for Black, nor is there any solace from White's strong first move, **1. Nc4!** (breaking in on d6; also possible is 1. Nf5, with a similar idea). Dead wrong now would be 1 . . . bxc4 2. Bxc4, which drives the Queen from posting over d7. After **1 . . . Rc7**, the rest of the game went **2. Nd6 Rb8 3. axb5 cxb5** (improving the scope of the Bishop but weakening key central squares) **4. Nxb7 Rbxb7 5. Qa2! Nb8 6. Na5 Qxa2 7. Rxa2 Ra7** (if 7 . . . Rd7 then 8. Rd5) **8. c6 Ra8 9. Rc2! Bxb4 10. Rd8+ Kg7 11. Bb6 Bxa5 12. Bxa5 Rxc6 13. Rxb8 Rxb8 14. Rxc6 b4 15. Bc7,** and **Black Resigned.**
1–0 (39)

Following The Yellow Brick Road

Though now Kasparov was playing fairly regularly, he had yet to cross swords with world champion Anatoly Karpov. This meeting was set for February 1981, when a special invitational team event was staged in Moscow in honor of the USSR Party Congress. Playing first board for the "Young Team," Kasparov pressed for attack against the champion, but Karpov's great defensive skill enabled him to draw both encounters. If before this minimatch Karpov had had doubts as to who would challenge him in the near future, there were fewer now. The only question that remained was whether Kasparov could cut his way through all the qualifying rounds to emerge as the official challenger. Still it was only a year before the interzonals would begin, and meanwhile there were many other events.

The Moscow Trade Show in April sponsored an international tournament of fourteen strong players, including Karpov, apparently at the height of his powers, who strolled into first with nine out of thirteen points. A full point and a half behind were

Kasparov, Polugaevsky, and a resurgent sixty-year-old Smyslov, all of whom were tied for second-through-fourth prizes. The individual game between the champion and Kasparov had ended in a draw, so the record between them so far was all even. During the tournament Kasparov celebrated his eighteenth birthday. The spindly little student from Botvinnik's school had grown into a strapping young man.

One month later, Kasparov was back in Moscow for the Soviet Republics Team Championship, representing his home province of Azerbaidzhan. Still another team event took him in August to Graz, Austria, for the under-twenty-six World Team Championship. Aided by Kasparov on first board and with the best individual performance, the USSR easily took top honors. Kasparov recalls: "I was happy with my play at Graz and was able to create a number of interesting games. The role of leader is undoubtedly an honored one, but at critical moments, a double responsibility lies on his shoulders. Therefore, I had to play for ten successive rounds without being substituted, and I was rested only in the final round, when the outcome of the tournament was already politically decided."

At Graz, American journalist Eric Schiller observed: "Gary's post mortems . . . were filled not with concrete variations [as often given by Fischer and Karpov], but with far more general reasoning."

Schiller added that "Garik's preparation just before the onset of the game is intense. Arriving early at the board, he plunges into deep concentration and starts to get his juices flowing. The face which was calm and peaceful only moments before becomes creased with tension. Sitting down opposite him, one can literally feel the pressure. He is, quite simply, frightening to play against.

"Away from the board, it is quite another matter, indeed. He enjoys blitz. . . . One evening he played a number of games against international masters on our [USA] team, and won them all, save a loss to Gurevich. . . . The consensus among some of America's finest blitz players [Fedorowicz, Gurevich, Benjamin, Kudrin] was that he is simply astounding."

After Graz followed the Interopolis at Tilburg in October, a super grandmaster tournament. For Kasparov, who had enjoyed an almost unbroken string of continuous successes, Tilburg must have seemed a severe setback. Gary sized up the tournament at the beginning and his results at the end: "Apart from the world champion and the challenger to his title [Victor Korchnoi], nearly all the world's leading players gathered in the small Dutch town of Tilburg for the fifth traditional tournament there." Any of the field's twelve grandmasters were capable of winning first prize.

"Regarding my comparative failure [Kasparov finished tied for sixth through eighth with an even score of three wins, three losses, and five draws] I can definitely say I was greatly let down by my inability to realize an advantage."

WHITE: **Smyslov**   TACTIC: **MATING ATTACK**
BLACK: **Kasparov**
WHERE: **USSR 1981**
ACTUAL POSITION

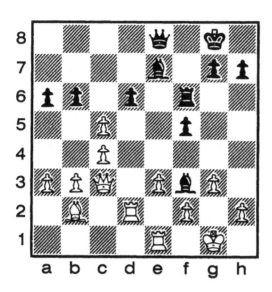

BLACK TO MOVE

ANALYSIS: After winning the exchange early in the game, the former world champ may have dozed off. Kasparov jarred him awake with **1 . . . Qh5!**, threatening 2 . . . Qxh2+, 3 . . . Rh6+, and Rh1 mate. So White tried **2. h4**, and the game went **2 . . . Qg4 3. Kh2** (to keep the Queen out of h3) **3 . . . bxc5!** (easy now, for 3 . . . Rg6 would allow White the possibility of exchanging Queens via 4. Qd4) **4. Rh1** (the only move, but it falls short) **4 . . . Rg6 5. Kg1 Bxh4 6. Qa5** (or 6. Rxd6 Bxg3 7. Rd8+ Kf7 8. Kf1 Bxf2, breaking and entering) **6 . . . h6!**, making a passage. All unglued before the coming . . . Bxg3, **White Resigned.** 0-1 (27)

WHITE: **Portisch** TACTIC: **PERPETUAL CHECK**
BLACK: **Kasparov**
WHERE: **Moscow 1981**
ACTUAL POSITION

BLACK TO MOVE

ANALYSIS: Two pawns down against Portisch, on the defensive the whole game, Kasparov espied a way to scrounge out a half point. He played **1 . . . Rxd2!**. After **2. Qxd2 Qf3+ 3. Qg2** (or 3. Rg2 Qf1+ 4. Rg1 Qf3+) **3 . . . Ng3+! 4. hxg3 Qh5+ 5. Qh2 Qf3+ 6. Rg2 Qd1+ 7. Qg1 Qh5+ 8. Rh2 Qf3+**, Portisch was convinced he couldn't win. One way or another, Black induces checks on d1, f3, and h5. **Drawn.**
Draw (49)

WHITE: Tukmakov   TACTIC: REMOVING THE GUARD
BLACK: Kasparov
WHERE: USSR 1981
ACTUAL POSITION

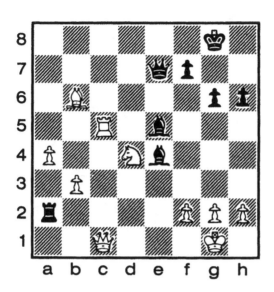

WHITE TO MOVE

ANALYSIS: White has connected passed pawns on the Queen-side but Black's two Bishops and well-posted Rook give him counterchances on the Kingside. In a difficult situation, Tukmakov blundered with **1. Qe3?**, and Kasparov could not miss the cruncher, **1 . . . Qxc5!**, when 2. Bxc5 leads to drowning by 2 . . . Ra1 +. By capturing the Rook at c5, Kasparov eliminated the possibility of a check-block at c1. **White Resigned.** With this victory, Kasparov tied for first in the Soviet championship with Lev Psakhis.
0–1 (29)

WHITE: **Kasparov**　　　　TACTIC: **MATING ATTACK**
BLACK: **Yurtaev**
WHERE: **USSR 1981**
ACTUAL POSITION

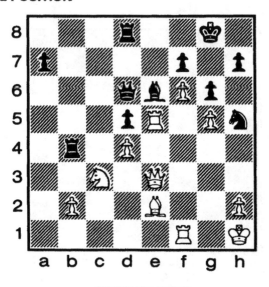

WHITE TO MOVE

ANALYSIS: Kasparov has mounted severe pressure against Black's Kingside, but has not yet breached the wall. The key is the razor sharp pawn at f6, cunningly poised to cut deeply into the Black fortress on cue. First the outer barrier was penetrated by the clearing **1. Bxh5 gxh5 2. g6!**, forcing **2 . . . hxg6** (2 . . . fxg6 hangs the Bishop at e6). The inner wall came down with **3. Rxe6!**, when 3 . . . Qxe6 would have led to 4. Qh6, and only 4 . . . Qxf6 could fend off immediate mate. So Black continued **3 . . . fxe6** (retaining the possibility of a subsequent shift of the Queen to f8 to guard g7, as well as opening the 2nd rank for a Rook to come to the King's aid), and the game ended **4. Qh6 Rb7**. Here **Black Resigned** rather than face the line 5. Qxg6+ Kh8 (5 . . . Kf8 loses to 6. f7, threatening 7. Qg8+) 6. f7 Qf8 (to avert 7. Qh6 mate) 7. Qxh5+ Kg7 8. Rg1+ Kf6 9. Qg5+ Kxf7 10. Rf1+ Ke8 11. Rxf8+ Kxf8 12. Qxd8+. A concisely executed denouement.
1–0 (30)

WHITE: **Kasparov**
BLACK: **Yurtaev**
WHERE: **USSR 1981**
POSSIBLE POSITION

TACTIC: **MATING ATTACK**

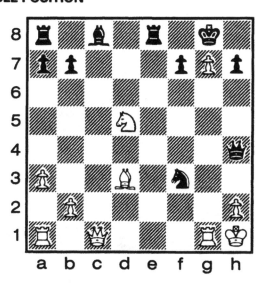

WHITE TO MOVE

ANALYSIS: Black can mate next move with Qxh2. But Kasparov has the surprise resource, **1. Qf4!**, defending the mate, attacking the Knight, and offering to trade Queens (threatening eventual Nf6 mate). Yet, instead of trading Queens after **1 . . . Qxf4**, the ingenious genius would have unleashed a stunning combination: **2. Ne7 + Rxe7** (forced) **3. Bxh7 + !** (as in a famous combination of Adolph Andersson's) **3 . . . Kxh7 4. g8/Q + Kh6 5. Qh8 mate**, where a series of three deflections (the Queen from h4, the Rook from e8 and the back rank, and the King from g8) were needed to promote the pawn. **White Wins.**
1–0 (30)

WHITE: **Kasparov**   TACTIC: **COUNTERATTACK**
BLACK: **Groszpeter**
WHERE: **Graz 1981**
POSSIBLE POSITION

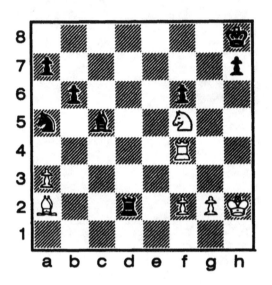

WHITE TO MOVE

ANALYSIS: The situation seems rosy for Black. He's up a pawn and on the verge of winning another, with his Rook and Bishop attacking multiple targets in White's camp. But Kasparov has the game-saving **1. Rg4!**, threatening 2. Rg8 mate. If Black defends by taking the Bishop 1 . . . Rxa2, then 2. Nh6 forces mate by either Rg8 or Nf7. And the defense 1 . . . Rd8 fails to 2. Nh6 Rf8 3. Nf7 + Rxf7 4. Bxf7, when White's Rook, Bishop, and King will eventually weave a mating net. **White Wins.**
Draw (30)

WHITE: **Kasparov**
BLACK: **Van der Weil**
WHERE: **Graz 1981**
POSSIBLE POSITION

TACTIC: **MATING ATTACK**

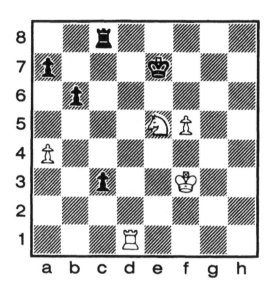

WHITE TO MOVE

ANALYSIS: Black, down a piece, could have tried to advance his c-pawn toward promotion. Gary stings him with **1. Rd7 +**. The consequences:

A) If the Black King comes up to f6, and the pawn is stopped after **2. Kf4** (threatening mate by Rf7 or Ng4) **2 . . . Rc4 +** (to divert the Knight) **3. Nxc4 c2** (threatening to Queen with check) **4. Rd6 +**, allowing a repositioning of the Rook. For example, if 4 . . . Ke7, then 5. Re6 +, followed by retreating the Rook to the first rank, stops the menacing march (in similar fashion, 4 . . . Kg7 is answered by 5. Rg6 + and 6. Rg1). And if 4 . . . Kf7 (instead of moving the King to g7 or e7), then 5. Ne5 + leads to 6. Rc6 and a comparable corraling of the looming c-monster.

B) If the King retreats to e8, then **2. f6 c2 3. Re7+ Kf8** (on 3 . . . Kd8, mate is executed by 4. Nf7) **4. Ng6+ Kg8 5. Rg7** constructs an Arabian mate. If Black tries in this line 2 . . . Rc5 instead of 2 . . . c2, then 3. f7+ Kf8 4. Rd8+ (or 4. Ng6+) promotes the pawn with check.

C) No better is withdrawing the King to f8, in that **2. f6 c2 3. Re7!** insures a needling Knight-check at g6 and a mating Rook-check at g7 to follow. **White Wins.**

1–0 (53)

WHITE: **Kasparov**   TACTIC: **MATING ATTACK**
BLACK: **Van der Weil**
WHERE: **Graz 1981**
POSSIBLE POSITION

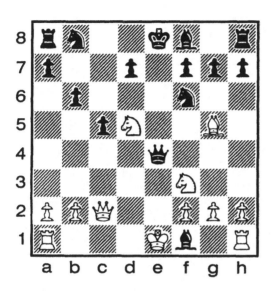

WHITE TO MOVE

ANALYSIS: If Black had so captured and checked on e4, Kasparov would have switched the on/off button with **1. Qxe4+**, when 1 . . . Nxe4 opens the g5-d8 diagonal and allows 2. Nc7 mate. **White Wins.** Black wisely declined this sudden death and the game went on.
1–0 (53)

WHITE: **Kasparov** TACTIC: **MATING ATTACK**
BLACK: **Fedorowicz**
WHERE: **Graz 1981**
ACTUAL POSITION

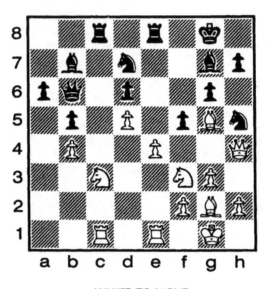

WHITE TO MOVE

ANALYSIS: Black has just shifted his Queen to apparent safety, retaining the threat to capture White's Knight on c3. With typical afflatus, Kasparov sensed his chance and brilliantly sacrificed a piece to craft a mating attack. The game continued **1. exf5!!**, a particularly apt sacrifice with Fedorowicz's time running out. Play went **1 . . . Rxe1+ 2. Rxe1 Bxc3** (2 . . . Rxc3 is answered by the unpleasant 3. Bd8, preparing the Queen's entrance at e7 and displaying extraordinary peripheral vision) **3. Re7 Rc4 4. Qh3** positioning for invasion along the h3-d7 diagonal) **4 . . . Bc8 5. fxg6 Ndf6** (5 . . . hxg6 is met by the encroaching 6. Qe6+) **6. Bxf6!** (so that 6 . . . Bxh3 permits 7. Re8 mate) **6 . . . Nxf6 7. gxh7+ Kf8** (7 . . . Kh8 flops to 8. Qh6) **8. h8/Q+ Kxe7 9. Qg7+**, and **Black Resigned**. The prospect of fending off two marauding Queens was more than Black bargained for.
1–0 (34)

WHITE: **Kasparov**   TACTIC: **CORRIDOR MATE**
BLACK: **Kouatly**
WHERE: **Graz 1981**
POSSIBLE POSITION

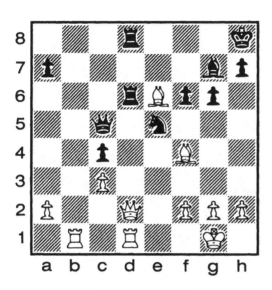

WHITE TO MOVE

ANALYSIS: This position results after Black's blunderous Rd7xd6?, avariciously capturing the passed d-pawn. In that case, White concludes matters pointedly with **1. Qxd6!**, when 1 . . . Qxd6 2. Rxd6 Rxd6 allows the back-ranking 3. Rb8 + and subsequent mate (3 . . . Rd8 4. Rxd8 + Bf8 5. Rxf8 + Kg7 6. Rg8). Nor is the recapture 1 . . . Rxd6 any better either, for 2. Rb8 + Rd8 3. Rdxd8! nullifies the potential Bishop-block on f8 (if 3 . . . Bf8, then 4. Rxf8 + Qxf8 5. Rxf8 + Kg7 6. Rg8 mate). Kasparov's play is fraught throughout with these sudden tactical turns. **White Wins.** Draw (25)

WHITE: **Miles**   TACTIC: **TRAPPED PIECE**
BLACK: **Kasparov**
WHERE: **Tilburg 1981**
POSSIBLE POSITION

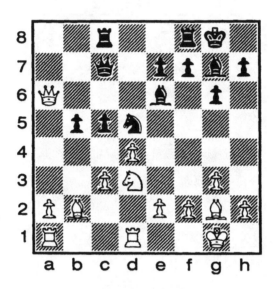

BLACK TO MOVE

ANALYSIS: This position would have happened if White had played 1. Qa4xa6? Though it seems to win a pawn, the capture actually results in the entrapment of White's Queen. Kasparov saw that, after **1 . . . Ra8 2. Qxb5 Ra5**, White must either lose his Queen or surrender a piece to extricate it. After the retreat 3. Qb3, White's Queen and Knight are vulnerable to the fork 3 . . . c4. And if 3. Qc4, then 3 . . . Nb6 lassoes her ladyship. **Black Wins.** In the actual game, Miles perceived this snare and retreated his Queen, drawing the game in 38 moves.
Draw (38)

WHITE: Kasparov
BLACK: Spassky
WHERE: Tilburg 1981
POSSIBLE POSITION

TACTIC: **PASSED PAWN**

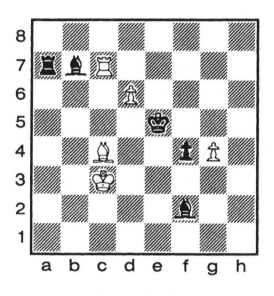

WHITE TO MOVE

ANALYSIS: In this deceptive position, Black has to play carefully, even though ahead by a Bishop for a pawn. If Spassky had thus centralized his King (Kf6-e5), Kasparov had a clever trick up his sleeve to regain the piece. After **1. d7**, threatening to Queen, **1 . . . Bh4** fails to **2. g5!**, when **2 . . . Bxg5** results in **3. Rc5+ Kd6** (to stop the pawn) **4. Rxg5. White Wins.** (The sure-footed Spassky avoided this pitfall with . . . Be4 instead of . . . Ke5, and went on to win.)

Golden Boy

Kasparov set to work correcting his shortcomings and only two months after Tilburg his efforts were rewarded: first equal with Lev Psakhis in the 49th USSR Championship at Frunze. Gold at last! In May of 1982 (Gary was now nineteen) another super tournament, this time in Bugojno, Yugoslavia. The uncertainties that dogged him at Tilburg were definitely gone. Dominating the tournament from beginning to end, Kasparov steamed into first place, one-and-a-half points ahead of Ljubojevic and Polugaevsky, whose eight points would ordinarily have been sufficient for victory.

With a FIDE rating of 2675, Gary was now the number two player in the world. Only the champion Karpov (2700) stood above him. The candidates cycle was now under way and the winner would emerge as Karpov's official challenger. Seeded into the Moscow interzonal on the basis of his high rating, Kasparov's chances were regarded as excellent. Neither his youth nor his relative inexperience would greatly handicap him, for Kasparov's sheer, raw talent was obvious to everyone. Yet no one, least of all Gary, could have predicted the obstacles that would be placed in his path.

After Bugojno came preparations for the Moscow interzonal, which was scheduled to start in September. Upon returning to the Foreign Languages Institute in Baku, where he was majoring in English, Gary had to sit for no less than five examinations in ten days. Chessically, however, everything was in order, thanks to Kasparov's team of supporters, which included Shakharov and Nikitin from the Botvinnik School, Vladimirov, and V. Chekhov. But in a short tournament like the Moscow tournament, where a paltry two of fourteen players move on to the next stage of the cycle, "only the players with the strongest nerves and the greatest physical fitness would triumph," according to Kasparov himself. So there was swimming, bicycling, and plenty of soccer, all to maintain stamina.

Moscow was the last of three interzonals to begin. On paper they all added up to even quality but in practice this was not so. Moscow's event was by far the strongest and the most bitterly contested. The percentage of wins tends to confirm this: Moscow—54 percent; Las Palmas—50.6 percent; and Toluca—46.2 percent. As for Kasparov, he started off reasonably well, but he was closely pursued by the Swede, Ulf Andersson. Their ninth-round game together marked a turning point. Here is Kasparov's description:

Ulf Andersson conducts splendidly his game from the 9th round. Victory appears to be close, but I manage to balance on the edge of the abyss . . . Black has acquired certain threats, for the parrying of which the ultra-cautious Swede requires time, and he has so little left! Ulf's indecision is aggravated by my offer of draw. In the end, the sight of the threateningly rising flag resolves all hesitation and Andersson signs the score sheet. [The game was drawn]. In effect, this signature symbolized his abandonment of any further battle in the tournament. Although the draw maintained the status quo of the two players, they approached the concluding four games in different psychological frames of mind. At the finish, I avoided losing any points [four wins], whereas Ulf drew all his games.

The cycle in November-December was interrupted for Kasparov. Two years had passed since the Malta Olympiad and the Soviet Federation wanted to field their most powerful team for

Lucerne. Both Karpov and Kasparov were to play, for the Soviets wanted no more surprises from the Hungarians. On this occasion there was no struggle. The USSR finished first, six-and-a-half points in front of the second-place Czech team. And the Hungarians—well, they were farther down the pack. As for Kasparov. he performed solidly at board two with six wins, five draws, and no losses.

WHITE: **Spassky**   TACTIC: **FORK**
BLACK: **Kasparov**
WHERE: **Bugojno 1982**
POSSIBLE POSITION

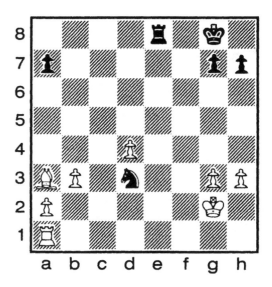

BLACK TO MOVE

ANALYSIS: If Spassky had brought out his Bishop in this way (Bc1-a3), Kasparov would have won at least the exchange by **1 ...** **Ne1+ 2. Kf2 Nc2**, forking the Bishop and the Rook. After 3. Bb2, Black simply takes the Rook. **Black Wins.**
Draw (32)

WHITE: **Kupreichik**   TACTIC: **PIN**
BLACK: **Kasparov**
WHERE: **USSR 1982**
ACTUAL POSITION

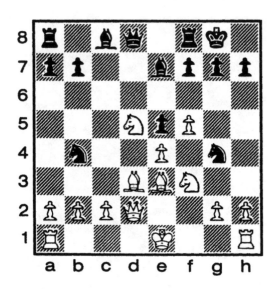

BLACK TO MOVE

ANALYSIS: Kasparov has just sacrificed his d-pawn for activity (1. Nc3xd5). Play continued **1 . . . Nxd5 2. exd5 e4!** (to open the e-file and the diagonals b8-h2 and f6-b2) **3. Bxe4 Re8!**, and White is faced with unpleasant possibilities:

A) He could attack the Black Knight with 4. h3. Play might then go 4 . . . Nxe3 5. Qxe3 Bb4 + ! (not 5 . . . Bh4 + 6. Kf1 Bxf5 7. Qf4 Bxe4 8. Nxh4 g5 9. Qg3 and White is still alive) 6. Kf1 (6. c3 comes to about the same thing) 6 . . . Bxf5 7. Ng5 (to defend the pinned Bishop) 7 . . . Bxe4 8. Nxe4 Qh4, and Black will exploit the deadly pin along the e-file.

B) He could castle Kingside with 4. 0-0. Black then seizes key channels with 4 . . . Bd6! 5. h3 Nxe3 6. Qxe3 Bxf5 7. Nd2 Qe7!, piling up on the pinned Bishop and threatening the pernicious 8 . . . Bc5, winning the White Queen.

C) He could castle Queenside **(4. 0-0-0)**. Here Black capitalizes with **4 . . . Bf6** 5. h3 (Kupreichik resigned himself to **5. Bg5 Rxe4** in the actual game) 5 . . . Nxe3 6. Qxe3 Bxf5 7. Nd2 Bg5!, winning at least the Bishop on e4 because of the subsequent pin on White's Knight after the Queen moves away. The example illustrates the power of Bishops and Rooks to effect pins on open boards, relatively uncluttered by hampering pawns. **Black Won.** 0–1 (30)

WHITE: **Kavalek**   TACTIC: **DEFLECTION**
BLACK: **Kasparov**
WHERE: **Bugojno 1982**
ACTUAL POSITION

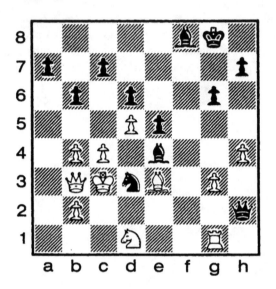

BLACK TO MOVE

ANALYSIS: White has a Rook for a Bishop and pawn, but his King is endangered and his pieces inharmoniously positioned. Kasparov consummated his initiative with **1 . . . Nc1!**, to which there was no satisfactory answer.

A) If White captures the Knight with 2. Bxc1, then 2 . . . Qxg1 regains the exchange and leaves Black a full pawn up. Furthermore, White must cope with the threat of Qd4 mate, leaving Kasparov time to devour the pawns on g3 and h4.

B) If White retrieves his Queen to the fourth rank (2. Qa4), then 2 . . . Na2+ 3. Kb3 (3. Qxa2 allows 3 . . . Qc2 mate) Bc2+ skewers White's Queen.

C) If White transfers his Queen along the third rank (2. Qa3), then 2 . . . Qc2 is mate. The primary theme throughout is the deflection of White's Queen from the defense of c2. **Black Won.** 0–1 (27)

WHITE: **Kasparov**
BLACK: **Belyavsky**
WHERE: **Moscow 1982**
POSSIBLE POSITION

TACTIC: **SKEWER**

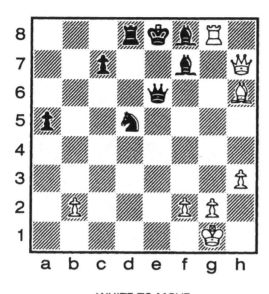

WHITE TO MOVE

ANALYSIS: Black is up two pieces for two pawns, but everything returns to an undismayed White—with interest. Play now continues **1. Rxf8+ Ke7 2. Rxf7+ Qxf7 3. Bg5+ Nf6 4. Bxf6+ Kxf6 5. Qh4+**, and the Rook at d8 falls. The resulting Queen endgame is a clear win for Kasparov. **White Wins.**
Draw (41)

WHITE: **Kasparov**   TACTIC: **DOUBLE ATTACK**
BLACK: **Belyavsky**
WHERE: **Moscow 1982**
POSSIBLE POSITION

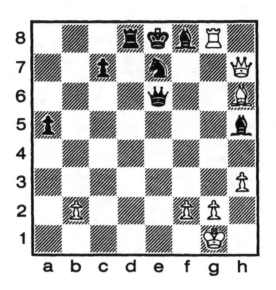

WHITE TO MOVE

ANALYSIS: White winds up regaining his sacrificed pieces with **1. Rxf8+ Kd7 2. Qd3+** (forcing a block on the d-file to avoid losing the Rook) **2 . . . Qd5** (2 . . . Qd6 stumbles into 3. Qb5+ and 4. Qxh5) **3. Qxd5+ Nxd5 4. Rf5!**, a fork that wins one of Black's minor pieces and leaves White with a two-pawn advantage. **White Wins.**
Draw (41)

WHITE: **Kasparov**
BLACK: **Sax**
WHERE: **Moscow 1982**
POSSIBLE POSITION

TACTIC: **PIN**

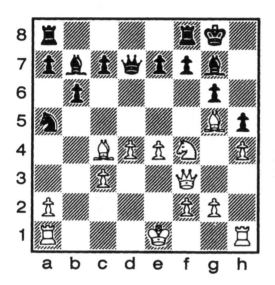

WHITE TO MOVE

ANALYSIS: White eyes a capture on g6 because of the feckless f-pawn, which, pinned by the Bishop on c4, cannot safeguard the target square. Black hopes that his last move (Nc6-a5) coerces White to first save his attacked Bishop. The surprise is **1. Nxg6!**, when **1 . . . Nxc4** fumbles to **2. Nxe7+ Kh7** (unless Black wants to dump his Queen with 2 . . . Qxe7 3. Bxe7) **3. Qxh5+ Bh6 4. Qxh6 mate**. Kasparov's vision and overall attack mastery have once again triumphed. **White Wins.**
1–0 (38)

WHITE: **Kasparov**   TACTIC: **IN-BETWEEN MOVE**
BLACK: **Sax**
WHERE: **Moscow 1982**

ACTUAL POSITION

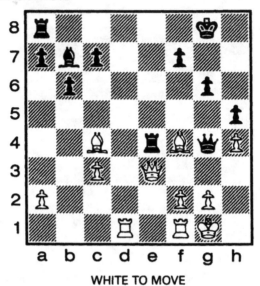

WHITE TO MOVE

ANALYSIS: Black's picture looks rather bright. He's up an extra pawn and is about to recoup his sacrificed piece, for White's Bishops are forked. But Kasparov has in mind a precise sequence of counterattacking moves. He plays **1. f3!**, when 1 . . . Rxe3 2. fxg4 enables him to retain his extra piece.

So Black parries with **1 . . . Qxf4**, stepping into **2. Bxf7 + ! Kg7** (2 . . . Kxf7 blows his Queen after 3. fxe4, creating an f-file pin, while 2 . . . Qxf7 loses at least the exchange to 3. fxe4) **3. Qd3!** (so that if the Rook retreats to safety, White can play 4. Qxg6 +) **3 . . . Qe3 +** (practically forced) **4. Qxe3 Rxe3 5. Rd7 Kh6 6. Rxc7,** and **White Won.** In this final position, White lost back his extra piece but is now superior by a pawn and comes away with a grip on the game.

Like other great attacking players, Kasparov continually proves that the best way to blunt an attack is to return extra material in exchange for other kinds of advantages.

1–0 (38)

WHITE: **Kasparov**   TACTIC: **MATING ATTACK**
BLACK: **Sax**
WHERE: **Moscow 1982**
ACTUAL POSITION

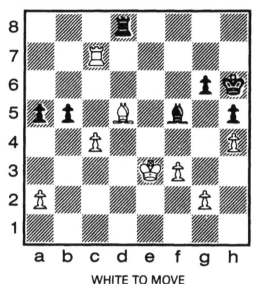

WHITE TO MOVE

ANALYSIS: Even in the endgame, where Queening a pawn is the main objective, Kasparov never loses sight of the enemy King. Here he played **1. Kf4**, centralizing his King as he prepares 2. g4, for delivering a fatal check on g5. In the event of 1 . . . bxc4 2. Bxc4 Rd4 +, Kasparov intended 3. Ke5! Rxh4 4. f4!. This virtually forces Black's Bishop to move to safety so that Sax can move his g-pawn. But 4 . . . Bb1 5. Bg8 (threatening mate on h7) 5 . . . g5 6. f5 g4 7. Kf6, and mate at h7 cannot be averted (7 . . . Bxf5 8. Kxf5 keeps the net in effect).

In the game Sax tried to anticipate these manipulations by 1 . . . **Bb1**, but after **2. g4** (threatening 3. g5 mate) **2 . . . hxg4 3. fxg4 Rf8 + 4. Kg3 Black Resigned**, since the prosaic 4 . . . g5 5. cxb5 must lose, there being no suitable way to contend with the juggernaut b-pawn.
1–0 (38)

WHITE: Korchnoi   TACTIC: **MATING ATTACK**
BLACK: Kasparov
WHERE: Lucerne 1982
POSSIBLE POSITION

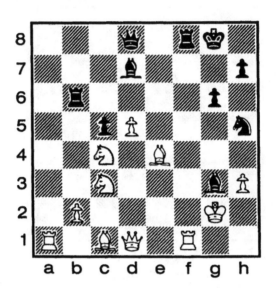

BLACK TO MOVE

ANALYSIS: Once again Kasparov must justify a piece sacrifice, and once again he does so with the crushing **1 . . . Bxh3 + !**, when **2. Kxh3** (2. Kg1 loses the Queen for starters to 2 . . . Rxf1 +) **2 . . . Qh4 + 3. Kg2 Qh2 mate. Black Wins.**
0–1 (36)

WHITE: Korchnoi   TACTIC: **TRAPPED PIECE**
BLACK: Kasparov
WHERE: Lucerne 1982
POSSIBLE POSITION

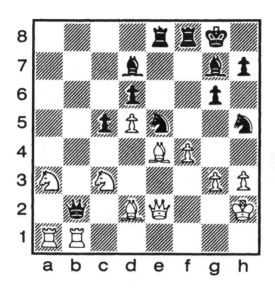

BLACK TO MOVE

ANALYSIS: The sky is dark for Kasparov's Queen, but the youngest World Champion ever has seen further. The adventuress is extricated by **1 . . . Nf3 + !**. If 2. Bxf3, then 2 . . . Rxe2 + is devastating; and if instead 2. Qxf3, then 2 . . . Qxd2 + will win material. **Black Wins.** One characteristic of a champion is wiliness.
0–1 (36)

WHITE: **Korchnoi**   TACTIC: **THE PIN**
BLACK: **Kasparov**
WHERE: **Lucerne 1982**
POSSIBLE POSITION

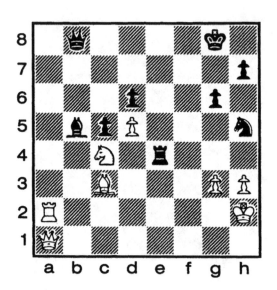

BLACK TO MOVE

ANALYSIS: White has just eluded a pin on his Knight by Qf1-a1. Though the Knight is still under attack, White threatens a counter-pin on Black's Queen with 2. Ra8. How does Kasparov deal with this threat? He ignores it and plays **1 . . . Bxc4** instead!

The pin **2. Ra8** is then answered by **2 . . . Re2+ 3. Kg1** (3. Kh1 permits 3 . . . Nxg3+) **3 . . . Rg2+!! 4. Kh1** (4. Kxg2 Bxd5+ concludes in the same way) **4 . . . Nxg3+ 5. Kxg2 Bxd5+**, and after the captures on g3 and a8 Black has three extra pawns. Kasparov's tactical wherewithal is staggering. **Black Wins.** 0–1 (36)

WHITE: Korchnoi   TACTIC: **MATING ATTACK**
BLACK: Kasparov
WHERE: Lucerne 1982
ACTUAL POSITION

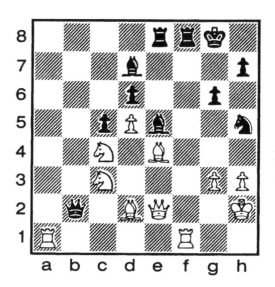

BLACK TO MOVE

ANALYSIS: Even though Black's Queen is attacked, it doesn't deter him from his ultimate objective, White's King. Kasparov volleyed **1 . . . Nxg3!**, threatening to be at least materially ahead after 2 . . . Nxe2 discovered check, even if his own Queen is captured first. So Korchnoi defended with **2. Rxf8 + Rxf8 3. Qe1** (in order to guard the Rook at a1) **3 . . . Nxe4 + 4. Kg2 Qc2 5. Nxe5** (essentially the only move, for 5. Qxe4 Qxe4 + 6. Nxe4 Bxa1 is decisive). Here we break with the game score. Kasparov played **5 . . . Rf2 +**, but after **6. Qxf2**, sacking the Queen to break the attack, it was still a hard game to win. Instead Kasparov might

have determined matters forthwith with 5 . . . Nxd2!. For example, 6. Nxd7 Nf3+ 7. Qe2 Nh4+! 8. Kg1 (of course 8. Kh2 Rf2+
might have a deleterious effect on White's health) 8 . . . Qxc3 9.
Qe6+ (else Black lifts the Rook at a1 with check) 9 . . . Kh8 10.
Nxf8 Qg3+! 11. Kf1 Qg2+ 12. Ke1 Nf3+ 13. Kd1 Qd2 mate.
Black Won.
0–1 (36)

WHITE: **Korchnoi**
BLACK: **Kasparov**
WHERE: **Lucerne 1982**
POSSIBLE POSITION

TACTIC: **MATING ATTACK**

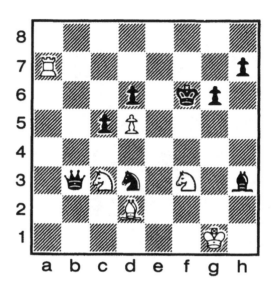

WHITE TO MOVE

ANALYSIS: Here we see Korchnoi with a chance to be tactically creative. At a definite material disadvantage, he could still turn the tables on Black with **1. Ne4+ Kf5 2. Nxd6+ Kg4** (2 . . . Kf6 3. Rf7 mate) **3. Nh2+ Kg3 4. Ne4+ Kh4 5. Rxh7 mate**. A native of wartime Leningrad, Korchnoi remains every inch a deadly fighter. **White Wins.**
0–1 (36)

WHITE: **Kasparov**　　　TACTIC: **KINGSIDE ATTACK**
BLACK: **Nunn**
WHERE: **Lucerne 1982**
ACTUAL POSITION

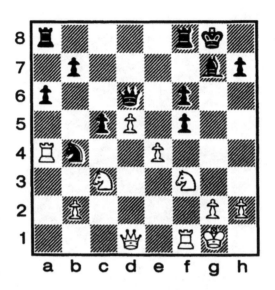

WHITE TO MOVE

ANALYSIS: White is a pawn behind, though Black's Kingside is in disarray and invites foray. Kasparov confronted Black with the jump **1. Nh4!**, threatening the damaging 2. Nxf5. After **1 . . . fxe4 2. Nf5 Qd7** (2 . . . Qe5 falters to 3. Qg4 Rf7 4. Nh6 +, winning at least the exchange) **3. Nxe4 Kh8** (3 . . . Rae8 4. Qg4 Kh8 5. Nxc5 jettisons the Knight at b4) **4. Nxc5**, White wins the exchange with **4 . . . Qxd5 5. Qxd5 Nxd5 6. Ne6**, forking the Rook and Bishop. **Black Resigned.**
1–0 (42)

WHITE: **Kasparov**
BLACK: **Suba**
WHERE: **Lucerne 1982**
POSSIBLE POSITION

TACTIC: **TRAPPED PIECE**

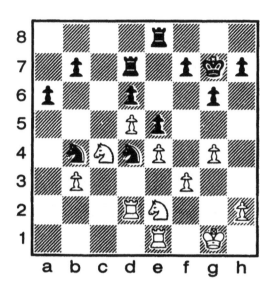

WHITE TO MOVE

ANALYSIS: Black might have inaugurated this line on the theory that after **1. Nxd4 exd4,** White cannot play 2. Rxd4 because of the fork on c2. But Kasparov blithely ignores the pawn and instead beleaguers the Knight on b4, which cannot safely retreat. The trick is **2. Ra1**, with the idea of 3. Ra4. If Black counters with 2 . . . f5, then 3. Ra4 fxe4 4. fxe4! and the Knight stays trapped while Black's potential passed pawns are sapped. Also unsatisfactory is 2 . . . d3 3. Ra4 Nc2 4. Rxd3 Ne1 5. Re3 Nc2 6. Rc3 Ne1 7. Kf2, and the Knight falls. **White Wins.**
1–0 (48)

WHITE: **Kasparov**   TACTIC: **WINNING THE EXCHANGE**
BLACK: **Suba**
WHERE: **Lucerne 1982**
POSSIBLE POSITION

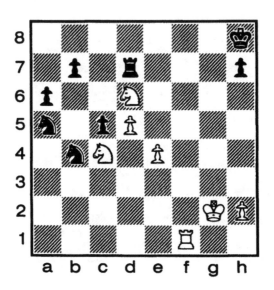

WHITE TO MOVE

ANALYSIS: Black has just captured a pawn on a5, thinking he would not lose in an exchange of Knights (1. Nxa5 Rxd6). White, however, cleverly interpolates **1. Ne8**. This saves the d6-Knight from attack and weaves a mating net (2. Rf8), while maintaining a possible capture of Black's hanging Knight at a5. One attempt at salvation is 1 . . . Rg7 + 2. Nxg7 Nxc4, but after 3. Rf7, Black is down the exchange with a losing position. **White Wins.**
1–0 (48)

WHITE: Kasparov TACTIC: **PASSED PAWN**
BLACK: Suba
WHERE: Lucerne 1982
ACTUAL POSITION

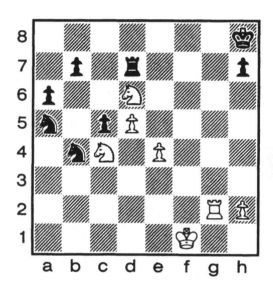

WHITE TO MOVE

ANALYSIS: With all of Black's fighting force amok to the left, White can prance on the right with **1. Ne5!**, when 1 . . . Rxd6 leaves Black chagrined by 2. Nf7 mate (thanks to White's long-armed Rook, which cuts down the g-file). With Black's Rook also assaulted, the only practical response is **1 . . . Rg7**, rescuing the Rook and providing an escape nook for the King. The game continued **2. Nef7+ Kg8 3. Nh6+ Kf8 4. Rf2+ Ke7 5. Nhf5+ Kd7 6. Nxb7!** (better than 6. Nxg7 Kxd6, when Black has slightly more spunk left in in his Queenside pawns) **6 . . . Nd3** (pieces and position hang by threads: note 6 . . . Nxb7 7. Nxg7 leaves White in control, a clear exchange ahead, with his center pawns intact) **7. Nxa5! Nxf2 8. Kxf2** (if 8. Nxg7 then 8 . . . Nxe4 breaks up White's center pawns and leads to a possible positional draw) **Rg4 9. Kf3 Rg1 10. e5 Rf1+ 11. Ke4 Re1+ 12. Kf4** and **Black Resigned.**

A rousing finale, with several unexpected turns. After operating on the Kingside, Kasparov—à la the legendary World Champion Alexander Alekhine (1892-1946)—suddenly switched to the Queenside (6. Nxb7!), and the Black Rook, seemingly doomed at g7, eked its way to the very end. Rook checks in the final position are futile, for White's King can hide in front of the Knight on f6. The computer-eyed Kasparov, through all the tactical strokes, never lost sight of his fundamental goal: the two connected passed pawns had to carry the day.

1–0 (48)

WHITE: Alburt   TACTIC: DISCOVERED ATTACK
BLACK: Kasparov
WHERE: Lucerne 1982
POSSIBLE POSITION

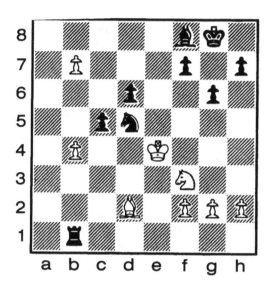

BLACK TO MOVE

ANALYSIS: Black's additional Rook will soon be nullified by White's new Queen if the b-pawn promotes, unless Black can cope with the new Queen. Black continues **1 . . . Nxb4!**, when **2. b8/Q** leads to the subsequent loss of her majesty by **2 . . . d5 +**. If either 3. Ke5 or 3. Kf4, then 3 . . . Nd3 + unleashes a winning Rook attack to b8. And if White instead answers 3. Ke3, then the Queen is won by the discovery 3 . . . Nc2 +. In both situations Kasparov stays an exchange and two pawns ahead. **Black Wins.** 0–1 (57)

WHITE: **Alburt**   TACTIC: **CORRIDOR MATE**
BLACK: **Kasparov**
WHERE: **Lucerne 1982**
POSSIBLE POSITION

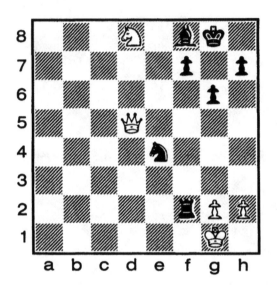

BLACK TO MOVE

ANALYSIS: In this materially balanced but asymmetrical position, Kasparov conjures a win with **1 . . . Rf5!**, when 2. Qxe4 flops to 2 . . . Bc5 + followed by an eventual back-rank mate on f1. White could present a stiff upper lip with 2. Qd1, though 2 . . . Bc5 + 3. Kh1 Nf2 + 4. Kg1 Nxd1 + 5. Kh1 Rf1 still evokes the *dum-dum-de-dum* of Chopin's funeral march. **Black Wins.**
0–1 (57)

WHITE: Alburt   TACTIC: PIN
BLACK: Kasparov
WHERE: Lucerne 1982
POSSIBLE POSITION

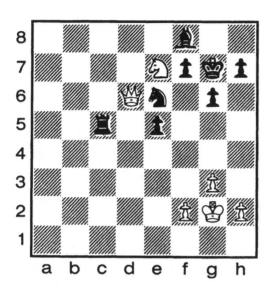

BLACK TO MOVE

ANALYSIS: White's misfortune is that his Knight is pinned to his Queen by Black's Bishop. Black's misfortune is that the immediate 1 . . . Rc7, piling up on the pinned horseman, collapses to 2. Qxe5+ and the pin is broken with a gain of time. Kasparov ascertains the correct procedure is to first play **1 . . . h5** and follow with **2 . . . Kh7**, then executing the Rook attack from c7. Against this creeping threat White has no useful defense. **Black Wins.** 0–1 (57)

WHITE: **Alburt**   TACTIC: **FORK**
BLACK: **Kasparov**
WHERE: **Lucerne 1982**

ACTUAL POSITION

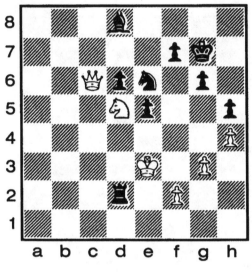

BLACK TO MOVE

ANALYSIS: Kasparov terminates White's hopes with **1 . . . Re2 + !**. If the King takes the Rook, then 2 . . . Nd4 + forks the royal house. So the 1984 and 1985 U.S. Champion continued **2. Kd3** and it was over after **2 . . . e4 + 3. Kc4** (3. Kc3 plunges into the same Knight-fork trick by 3 . . . Rc2 +, except here the skewer forces White to take the Rook) **3 . . . Rc2 + 4. Nc3 Bf6 5. Qxe4 Rxc3 + 6. Kd5 Rc5 + 7. Kxd6 Be5 +. White Resigned** rather than face the firing squad of 8. Kd7 (8. Qxe5 merely leaves White a piece down after 8 . . . Rxe5 9. Kxe5) 8 . . . Rc7 + 9. Ke8 Bd6, threatening the King-pillaging 10 . . . Re7 mate. Ten-move, sustained attacking variations are Kasparov's caviar.
0–1 (57)

WHITE: Kasparov   TACTIC: COUNTERATTACK
BLACK: Gligoric
WHERE: Lucerne 1982
POSSIBLE POSITION

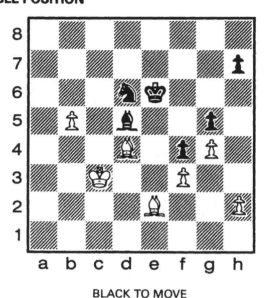

BLACK TO MOVE

ANALYSIS: White has a passed b-pawn and two Bishops opposing a Bishop and Knight. These are normally significant endgame advantages. But Black has unexpected game-saving ammunition. Correct is **1 . . . h5!!**. This sparkling sacrifice effects the necessary breakthrough.

A) White can take the pawn 2. gxh5 Bxf3! (to divert the Bishop from defense of b5) 3. Bxf3 Nxb5+ 4. Kd3 Nxd4 5. Kxd4, and Black draws by retreating his King toward h8. Since White's Bishop does not influence the dark-square corner, White is up the creek with a positional draw, unable to close in without delivering stalemate.

B) White can defend with his h-pawn: 2. h3 hxg4 3. hxg4 Nxb5+! 4. Bxb5 Bxf3 5. Ba6 (trying for Bc8) 5 . . . Kd7!, and after 6 . . . Bxg4, White, divested of pawns, cannot win. Should be a **Draw.**

1–0 (51)

6

THE STARS AND BEYOND

In February and March of 1983 Kasparov played excellent chess to win his quarterfinal match with Belyavsky, and the way to the summer semifinal with Korchnoi in Pasadena seemed clear. But now politics intervened. Boycotting the Los Angeles Summer Olympic Games, the Soviet Union was not about to soften and send one lone chessplayer to California. Korchnoi showed up, played one move, **1. d4**, but there was no Kasparov. Declared loser by forfeit, Kasparov seemed stopped in his tracks. Yes, there were maneuvers behind the scenes to get the match back on track, but Kasparov played no part in them.

About this period of limbo Kasparov writes: "The complete uncertainty which had arisen concerning the Candidates Semi-Final Matches forced me to reconsider my plans. It was evident that there was only one way out of this state of 'chess weight-lessness'—to participate in an international tournament. Therefore the invitation from Yugoslavia, which arrived precisely at that time, was accepted without hesitation."

The tournament at Niksic, an event as star-studded as Tilburg and Bugojno, was dedicated on this occasion to the great Yugoslavian grandmaster, Svetozar Gligoric, on his sixtieth birthday. Kasparov's instincts about playing were quite right. Vaulting into the lead, he never looked back, turning in the kind of performance that had not been seen since the days of Bobby Fischer's domination. The prospect of the Candidates Matches continuing without Kasparov was made to look ridiculous. But afterward a compromise of sorts was worked out and the match with Korchnoi was on again, this time set for London at the end of 1983.

Prior to the match, Korchnoi described his opponent's chess: "Kasparov is a player with a single knockout blow. But if you can successfully parry his fierce attacks and be the first to land a blow, Kasparov may lose his confidence and become unsteady." At the midway point of the match it appeared that the immensely experienced Korchnoi had discovered the answer. Deftly parrying his opponent's moves, he won the first game and drew the next four. Kasparov certainly was not in his happiest frame of mind.

On the morning of December 4, the day of the sixth game, a sleepy Kasparov received a long-distance call from Moscow. It was Botvinnik, asking his former student to remember what happened in the 1933 match between Botvinnik and Salo Flohr. Kasparov recalled that Botvinnik had lost the first and sixth games but then came back to win the ninth and tenth. "Well now," said Botvinnik, "see what a favorable position you are in. You haven't lost the sixth game." Then he added, "But in general everything is all right. A little self-discipline and you should win the match."

This encouraging chat with his chess mentor immediately buoyed Kasparov's spirits and the next four games proved to be a disaster for Korchnoi. Three wins for Kasparov and just one draw for Korchnoi. The knockout blow had been landed! At game eleven the match was ended; a 7-4 victory over the player who perhaps was the strongest *never* to have won the world championship.

WHITE: **Belyavsky**　　　　TACTIC: **DISCOVERED CHECK**
BLACK: **Kasparov**
WHERE: **Moscow 1983, Match Game 2**
POSSIBLE POSITION

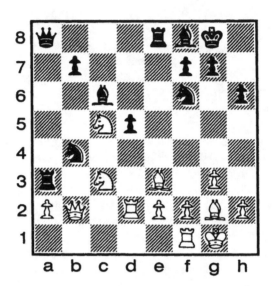

BLACK TO MOVE

ANALYSIS: Kasparov speedily discerns that two pawns must be shoved to discover a winning attack. It begins with **1 . . . d4!**, clearing the c6-g2 diagonal with a gain of time, for 2. Bxc6 loses a piece to the interpolated 2 . . . dxc3 followed by recapturing White's light-squared Bishop. If White answers naturally with 2. Bxd4, Black filches a Knight by 2 . . . Bxg2 3. Kxg2 b6 +, pocketing the Knight at c5 because of the discovered check along the a8-g2 line. In this impressive example of Kasparov's radar vision, three Black units had to be eliminated from the key diagonal and White's King forced onto an unfavorable square. **Black Wins.** 0–1 (38)

WHITE: Belyavsky   TACTIC: COUNTERATTACK
BLACK: Kasparov
WHERE: Moscow 1983, Match Game 2
POSSIBLE POSITION

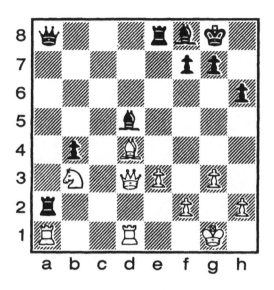

WHITE TO MOVE

ANALYSIS: White feels that Black's overworked Queen is guarding too many men, namely the Rook at a2 and the Bishop at d5, and deems that playing **1. Bxg7?** will bring 1 . . . Bxg7 2. Rxa2 Qxa2 3. Qxd5. But Black is unpersuaded and plays the game-saving **1 . . . Bh1!**. However White may grapple with the mate threat at g2, his position is flagrantly indefensible. **Black Wins.** 0–1 (38)

WHITE: **Belyavsky**   TACTIC: **MATING NET**
BLACK: **Kasparov**
WHERE: **Moscow 1983, Match Game 2**
POSSIBLE POSITION

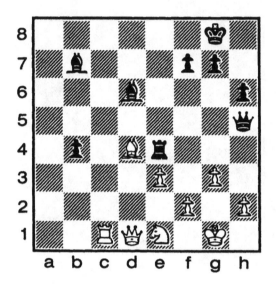

BLACK TO MOVE

ANALYSIS: With g2 guarded by the Knight and White on the verge of trading Queens, White's position seems tenable. But Kasparov wills a way to mate, evinced after **1 . . . Qxh2 +! 2. Kxh2 Rh4 +**, when the Rook is immune from capture because the g-pawn is pinned. Thus 3. Kg1 Rh1 is mate. **Black Wins.** 0–1 (38)

WHITE: Belyavsky   TACTIC: **MATING ATTACK**
BLACK: Kasparov
WHERE: Moscow 1983, Match Game 4
POSSIBLE POSITION

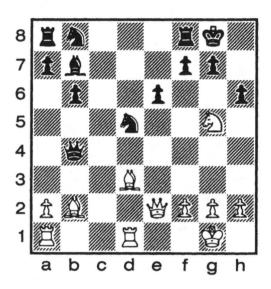

WHITE TO MOVE

ANALYSIS: This was Belyavsky's game to win. With five pieces poised for the kill on an open board (no pawns blocking passage through the center), White has terrific attacking possibilities. The *putsch* begins: **1. Qe5** (threatening mate at g7) **1 . . . Nf6** (1 . . . f6 2. Qxe6+ Kh8 3. Qf5 is bad for Black's health) **2. Bh7+** (2 . . . Nxh7 3. Qxg7 mate) **2 . . . Kh8 3. Qxf6! gxf6 4. Bxf6 mate**. Even an attacking phenomenon can overextend himself and get mated. Even giants are slaughtered sometimes. **White Wins.**
1–0 (38)

WHITE: **Belyavsky**   TACTIC: **MATING ATTACK**
BLACK: **Kasparov**
WHERE: **Moscow 1983, Match Game 4**
POSSIBLE POSITION

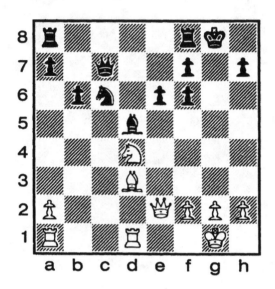

WHITE TO MOVE

ANALYSIS: The kinky problem here is that Black's position is exposed on the Kingside and his pieces are displaced toward the Queenside. White could pierce the thinning epidermis with **1. Bxh7 + !**, when **1 . . . Kxh7** (or 1 . . . Kh8 2. Qh5 and White will shortly mate) **2. Qh5 + Kg8 3. Qg4 + Kh8 4. Rd3** is a killer. Only an earthquake can stop White's Rook from delivering mate at h3. **White Wins.**
1–0 (38)

WHITE: **Belyavsky**   TACTIC: **MATING ATTACK**
BLACK: **Kasparov**
WHERE: **Moscow 1983, Match Game 4**
POSSIBLE POSITION

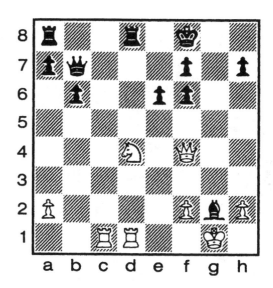

WHITE TO MOVE

ANALYSIS: Black seems to have counterplay, but White's attack is already there. The hailstorm starts with **1. Nxe6 + !**. After **1 . . . fxe6 2. Qxf6 + Ke8** (on 2 . . . Kg8 White cleans up with 3. Rxd8 + Rxd8 4. Qxd8 + Kf7 5. Rc7 +) **3. Qxe6 + Kf8** (or 3 . . . Qe7 4. Qg8 + Qf8 5. Re1 + Kd7 6. Qxh7 + Kd6 7. Qc7 + Kd5 8. Rcd1 mate) **4. Qf6 + Ke8 5. Re1 + Be4 6. Rc4**, White regains his piece with a crushing attack. **White Wins.**
1–0 (38)

WHITE: **Belyavsky**   TACTIC: **IN-BETWEEN CHECK**
BLACK: **Kasparov**
WHERE: **Moscow 1983, Match Game 4**
POSSIBLE POSITION

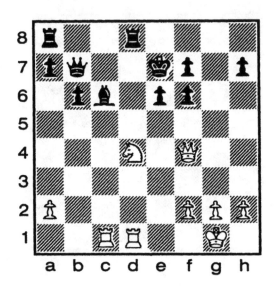

WHITE TO MOVE

ANALYSIS: While 1. Nxc6+ fails to 1 . . . Qxc6!, when 2. Rxc6 loses to 2 . . . Rxd1 mate, the capture **1. Rxc6** succeeds, for the counter-capture **1 . . . Rxd4** (hoping for 2. Rxd4 Qxc6) can be answered by the in-between check (or *zwischenzug*) **2. Rc7+**. After Black moves his King (or enters upon 2 . . . Qxc7 3. Qxc7+ K moves 4. Rxd4) White can respond **3. Rxd4**, leaving him a Rook ahead. **White Wins.**
1–0 (38)

WHITE: **Belyavsky**   TACTIC: **PIN**
BLACK: **Kasparov**
WHERE: **Moscow 1983, Match Game 4**
POSSIBLE POSITION

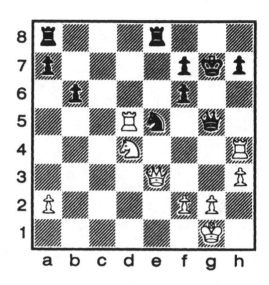

WHITE TO MOVE

ANALYSIS: At f5 Black's Queen was in the pan, at g5 it's in the fire. The simple **1. Rg4** pins the consort to the King. The apparent defense 1 . . . Nxg4 doesn't cut the mustard because the move unleashes the other Rook, allowing 2. Rxg5 + . One way or the other, the empress goes. **White Wins.**
1–0 (38)

WHITE: **Belyavsky** TACTIC: **DISCOVERED ATTACK**
BLACK: **Kasparov**
WHERE: **Moscow 1983, Match Game 4**
POSSIBLE POSITION

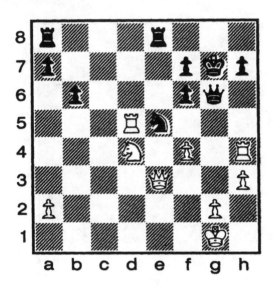

BLACK TO MOVE

ANALYSIS: White's last move (f4) purported to drive away Black's resources for a Kingside defense. However, it proves ineffectual. After **1 . . . Qb1 + 2. Kh2** (2. Kf2 runs into something similar) **2 . . . Ng6** (not 2 . . . Ng4 +, uncovering an attack to the Queen, because White then captures the Knight with check, 3. Rxg4) **3. Qg3**, White has saved his Queen and Rook but now the King gets harassed. The atom-splitter is **3 . . . Re1 4. Qg4** (giving the King a loophole) **4 . . . Rh1 + 5. Kg3 Qe1 + 6.Kf3 Rf1 mate**. A symbiotic Queen and Rook can be an awesome force for good or evil. **Black Wins.**
1–0 (38)

WHITE: Kasparov   TACTIC: **PASSED PAWN**
BLACK: Belyavsky
WHERE: Moscow 1983, Match Game 5
POSSIBLE POSITION

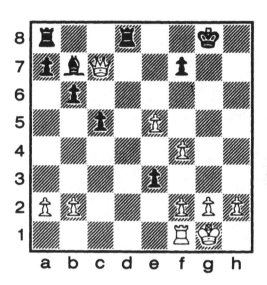

BLACK TO MOVE

ANALYSIS: In this wild and woolly phantasmagoria, Kasparov's marauding Queen could easily have bitten off too much to chew after 1. QxN(c7)?. The shooting star is **1 . . . e2.** If **2. Re1,** then **2 . . . Rd1** is downright debilitating. Little aid is offered by 2. Qxb7, for 2 . . . Rd1 (stronger than 2 . . . exf1/Q +) 3. Qxa8 + Kg7 and **Black Wins.**
1–0 (38)

WHITE: **Kasparov**   TACTIC: **DOUBLE ATTACK**
BLACK: **Belyavsky**
WHERE: **Moscow 1983, Match Game 5**
ACTUAL POSITION

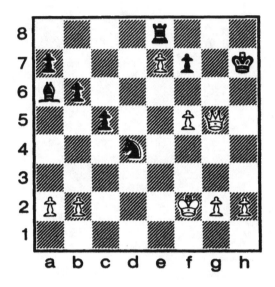

WHITE TO MOVE

ANALYSIS: Across the board, Black's united pieces prove ineffectual against White's officious Queen and ferocious pawns. Belyavsky's unhinging was **1. f6** (threatening 2. Qg7 mate) **1 . . . Ne6 2. Qh5+ Kg8 3. Qg4+ Kh7 4. Qa4** (forking the Bishop and Rook) **Nc7 5. Qd7 Rc8 6. Qf5+**, and mate follows:

A) 6 . . . Kh8 7. Qh5+ Kg8 8. Qg5+ Kh7 9. Qg7.

B) 6 . . . Kh6 7. g4, and White's Queen mates at h5. **White Wins.**

Kasparov surefootedly evaded all the snares, and loped home to victory.

1–0 (38)

WHITE: **Kasparov**   TACTIC: **PIN**
BLACK: **Belyavsky**
WHERE: **Moscow 1983, Match Game 7**
POSSIBLE POSITION

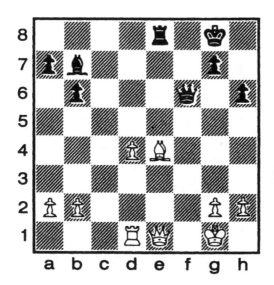

WHITE TO MOVE

ANALYSIS: Of White's two checks that give a discovered attack to the Rook, the strongest is **1. Bd5+!**. White's Bishop is immune because Black's Rook hangs to White's Queen. After **1 ... Kf8**, to protect his Rook, White continues the hunt with **2. Qb4+**. Black has two options:

A) He can play 2 . . . Re7, losing his Bishop (3. Bxb7—3.Rf1 wins the Black Queen, but gives up a Rook and Bishop and is therefore not as good).

B) He can play 2 . . . Qe7, which allows mate (3. Rf1).

White Wins.

Draw (21)

WHITE: **Kasparov**   TACTIC: **PASSED PAWN**
BLACK: **Belyavsky**
WHERE: **Moscow 1983, Match Game 7**
POSSIBLE POSITION

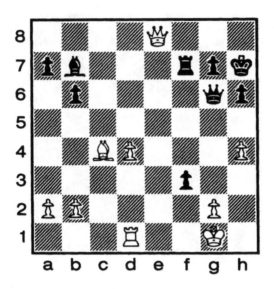

WHITE TO MOVE

ANALYSIS: In this possible variation, could Kasparov have stopped the mate threat at g2 by pinning the Black Queen with **1. Bd3?** No, because Black still comes out on top after **1 . . . f2+ 2. Kh2** (on 2. Kf1 Black wins by 2 . . . Bxg2+) **2 . . . Qxd3!**, leaving Belyavsky a piece ahead after the pawn promotes. **Black Wins.** Draw (21)

WHITE: Belyavsky   TACTIC: REMOVING THE GUARD
BLACK: Kasparov
WHERE: Moscow 1983, Match Game 8
POSSIBLE POSITION

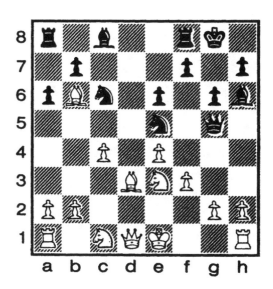

BLACK TO MOVE

ANALYSIS: All looks hunky-dory for White, with his Knight at e3 guarded by the Bishop at b6 and his g-pawn protected by the Knight. But Kasparov insidiously challenges the Bishop with **1 . . . Nd7**. If White protects it by 2. c5, leaving his Knight helpless, Black takes it, 2 . . . Qxe3 +. If White protects the Bishop instead with his Queen, 2. Qb3, then 2 . . . Nxb6 3. Qxb6 leads to 3 . . . Qxe3 +. 4. Qxe3 Bxe3, again acquiring a piece. Since the Bishop has no secure retreating square along the a7-e3 diagonal, either the Bishop or Knight must go. **Black Wins.**
0–1 (46)

WHITE: **Belyavsky**   TACTIC: **PASSED PAWN**
BLACK: **Kasparov**
WHERE: **Moscow 1983, Match Game 8**
POSSIBLE POSITION

BLACK TO MOVE

ANALYSIS: In this wide-open position, Black's Bishops and passed pawn impend like Damocles' sword. Kasparov charges ahead with **1 . . . Qxf4!!**. After **2. Rxf4 Bxf4 3. Rxe8** (on 3. Qxf4 Rxe1 + 4. Bf1 Bd3 scores the point, while 3. Qf2 Rxe1 + 4. Qxe1 Bxd3 rewards Black with two Bishops and a Rook against the lone Queen) **3 . . . Bxg3 4. Rxf8+ Kxf8 5. Bxf5 gxf5 6. hxg3 d3**, and the confident footman puffs into Queenland. **Black Wins.** 0–1 (46)

WHITE: Ljubojevic   TACTIC: KINGSIDE ATTACK
BLACK: Kasparov
WHERE: Niksic 1983
ACTUAL POSITION

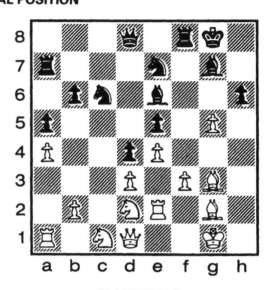

BLACK TO MOVE

ANALYSIS: White is badly hemmed in. His pieces, confined to the first two ranks, are bumpety-bump. Only the Bishop at g3 leans out on the third rank. Naturally, Kasparov focuses on the White King, unsheltered by pawn cover. The g-file and the outpost square f4 are the paths of attack. The debacle begins **1 . . . Ng6! 2. gxh6.** Since White has no constructive ideas, he chews up a few loose pawns. But now Kasparov can hinge the h6-d2 diagonal to his growing arsenal. And the pressure mounts: **2 . . . Bxh6 3. Nf1 Rg7.** There's no end of new fuel for an accomplished attack master. Here it's a Queenside Rook suddenly leaping across the board, behind the lines. White's **4. Rf2** is met by **4 . . . Be3!**, when 5. Nxe3 dxe3 6. Rf1 Qg5 7. Ne2 Nf4 bombards victory. So White abandons the exchange with **5. b3**, and Black momentarily declines with **5 . . . Nf4.** Stuffed to the gills with all this, **White Resigned.**
0–1 (25)

WHITE: **Kasparov**   TACTIC: **MATING ATTACK**
BLACK: **Petrosian**
WHERE: **Niksic 1983**
ACTUAL POSITION

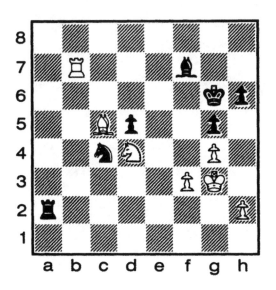

WHITE TO MOVE

ANALYSIS: How do you win an ending with a mere handful of pieces and no passed pawn to work with? "No problem," replied Kasparov. "I just play for mate." To wit, Kasparov continued **1. Nf5**. This tightens the cordon around Black's King. Now the Bishop at f7 cannot budge. For example, if 1 . . . Be6 (or 1 . . . Be8), then 2. Bd4 Bf7 3. Ne7+ Kh7 4. Rb8, with mate following on h8.

Or Black could try the counterattack 1 . . . Nd2, threatening 2 . . . Nf1+ and 3 . . . Rxh2 mate, but that fails against 2. Rb6+ Kh7 3. Rxh6+ Kg8 4. Bd6!. With h2 held, White will threaten 5. Be5 and 6. Rh8 mate, which should win, with best play.

So Black responded with **1 . . . Ra6**. Kasparov pressed his

advantage with **2. h4!**, auguring 3. h5 + Kf6 4. Bd4 + Ke6 (or 4 . . . Ne5 5. Bxe5 + Kxe5 6. Rxf7) 5. Re7 mate. So Black grabbed the usurper **2 . . . gxh4 +**, which led to **3. Nxh4 + Kg7** (or 3 . . . Kf6 4. Bd4 + Ke6 5. Nf5, and Black hangs by his thumbs) **4. Nf5 + Kg6** (4 . . . Kg8 meets 5. Nxh6 +) **5. Bd4.** Here **Black Resigned**. A possible conclusion is 5 . . . Nd6 (as good as any) 6. Nxd6 Rxd6 7. f4, threatening 8. f5 + and 9. Rxf7. Should Black try to move his Bishop to safety, White then mates at g7 with his Rook.
1–0 (51)

WHITE: **Timman**   TACTIC: **DISCOVERED ATTACK**
BLACK: **Kasparov**
WHERE: **Niksic 1983**
POSSIBLE POSITION

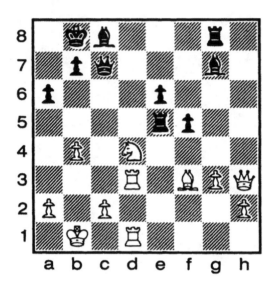

BLACK TO MOVE

ANALYSIS: White's Queenside is so loose, a mere exchange sacrifice can spearhead the breakthrough. Kasparov played **1 . . . Re4!**, so the b-pawn hangs if the Knight zips out of attack. Timman tried **2. c3** (2. a3 Rxd4! 3. Rxd4 e5, and when the Rook moves, Black pushes 4 . . . e4, eyeing 5 . . . Qc3 or 5 . . . Qe5. Or, if White captures the Rook 2. Bxe4, then 2 . . . fxe4 followed by 3 . . . Bxd4 and 4 . . . e5 discovers an attack on White's Queen and secures a piece). After 2. c3, play continued **2 . . . e5 3. Nb3 Rc4 4. Bd5 Rh8 5. Qg2 Rxc3**, and Black has regained his pawn with much the better position. **Black Wins.**
0–1 (66)

WHITE: Larsen   TACTIC: PIN
BLACK: Kasparov
WHERE: Niksic 1983
POSSIBLE POSITION

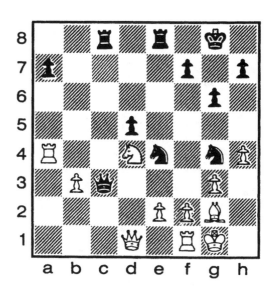

BLACK TO MOVE

ANALYSIS: Together, Black's Knights and Queen make an assault force to cause tremors. Several possibilities loom, the most invincible being **1 . . . Nexf2! 2. Rxf2 Qe3**, and Black regains the material with interest. If White in doubt plays **3. Qf1** (or 3. Qe1), then **3 . . . Rc1** claims the Queen by a different pin. **Black Wins.** 0–1 (56)

WHITE: **Larsen**
BLACK: **Kasparov**
WHERE: **Niksic 1983**
ACTUAL POSITION

TACTIC: **PASSED PAWN**

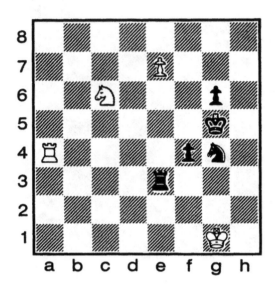

WHITE TO MOVE

ANALYSIS: This problem-ridden position, actually enacted at the board, could double as an endgame study. With best play it appears that Larsen could have managed a draw. As it was, Kasparov's narrow victory was hardly a cinch.

White played **1. Ra5 + ?**. Larsen intended to follow with either 2. Ne5 or 2. Re5, messing up the Black Rook's control of the Queening square e8, but also encouraging Black's King to cozy nearer White's with a gain of time. Here the minus outweighs the plus. The most feasible move, however, is 1. Ra8. Unhappily, it clashes with 1 . . . Re1 + 2. Kg2 Re2 + 3. Kf1 f3! 4. e8/Q Nh2 + 5. Kg1 f2 +, Queening with check the next move.

Also clever is to commence with 1. Ne5, when 1 . . . Rxe5 leads to the pin 2. Ra5, preventing Black's Rook from capturing the pawn. Nonetheless, after 2 . . . Rxa5 3. e8/Q Rf5, White still has plenty of work cut out for him, for Black can't lose.

The key to a draw was the paradoxical *1. Nd4!!*. This dexterous resource was found by the Dutchman Jan Timman in the post mortem. The two main lines are:

A) 1 . . . Rxe7 2. Nf3 + Kf5 3. Nh4 + Kf6 4. Rxf4 + Kg5 5. Nxg6, eliminating Black's last pawn.

B) 1 . . . Nf6 2. Ra6! Rxe7 3. Ne6 + Kf5 4. Nxf4, reducing to an ending which should be a draw with correct play.

In the actual game, Black answered **1. Ra5 +** with **1 . . . Kh4**. White then presented **2. Ra8**, for 2. Ne5 (or 2. Re5) doesn't work after 2 . . . Nxe5 3. e8/Q Re1 + 4. Kg2 (not 4. Kf2 Nd3 + discovering on the new Queen) 4 . . . f3 + 5. Kf2 (and not 5. Kh2 because of 5 . . . Ng4 mate) 5 . . . Nd3 +.

After **2. Ra8** Black defended with **2 . . . Nf6**. Play continued **3. Kg2** (instead of 3. Rf8 Kg3, portending mate) **3 . . . f3 + 4. Kf1 Kg3 5. Nd4** (no better is 5. Rf8 Ng4 6. e8/Q Nh2 + 7. Kg1 Rxe8) **5 . . . Ng4 6. Nxf3 Rxf3 + 7. Kg1** (7. Ke1 Re3 +) **7 . . . Nh2!**, threatening 8 . . . Rf1 mate (But not 7 . . . Nf2, because of 8. Rh8—to stop 8 . . . Nh3—8 . . . Ra3 9. Kf1!, and White is all right). White replied to **7 . . . Nh2!** with **8. Rf8**, but after **8 . . . Rc3** White gave up in view of 9. Rf1 Re3, catching the e-pawn. On any other ninth move for White, Black mates. A real cliffhanger. **White Resigned.**

0–1 (56)

WHITE: **Nikolic**   TACTIC: **PIN**
BLACK: **Kasparov**
WHERE: **Niksic 1983**

ACTUAL POSITION

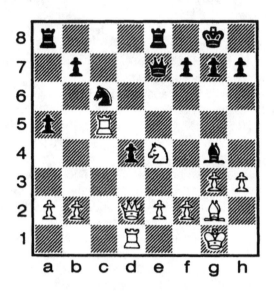

BLACK TO MOVE

ANALYSIS: In this open position, Black's double pressure on the e-file and restraining isolated d-pawn give him a cloudless spatial advantage. White's blunderous last move (h3), rather than driving away the pesky Bishop, allows Black to steal the troubled e-pawn. Kasparov cashed in **1 . . . Bxe2!**, for the recapture **2. Qxe2** drops the exchange to 2 . . . Qxc5, for 3. Nxc5 results in 3 . . . Rxe2. The predator is always keen to the hunt. **Black Won.** 0–1 (71)

WHITE: **Miles**
BLACK: **Kasparov**
WHERE: **Niksic 1983**
POSSIBLE POSITION

TACTIC: **MATING ATTACK**

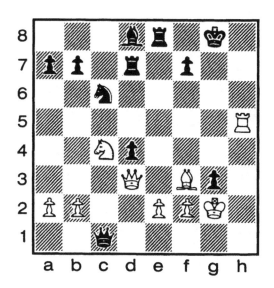

WHITE TO MOVE

ANALYSIS: Down by a Rook, White uncorks some legerdemain. By removing control of e5 with **1. Bxc6 bxc6**, he could mate after 2. Qh7 + Kf8 4. Qh8 + Ke7 5. Re5. **White Wins.** Kasparov nimbly avoided this line and the actual game ended in a draw. Note how Kasparov in this isolated d-pawn position could have put similar pressure against White's e-pawn, as in the Nikolic-Kasparov game from the same tournament (preceding page). In both examples, a major Black piece occupies the half-open e-file and Black's d-pawn restrains White's e-pawn.
Draw (40)

WHITE: **Seirawan**   TACTIC: **TRIANGULATION**
BLACK: **Kasparov**
WHERE: **Niksic 1983**

ACTUAL POSITION

WHITE TO MOVE

ANALYSIS: The last move of the time control has Seirawan making the decisive error in a pure King-and-pawn endgame. White played **1.e4?**. A better move would have been 1. Kd4, centralizing his King and restraining Black's progress. For example:

A) 1 . . . f5 2. f4 a5 3. e4 fxe4 4. Kxe4 Kc5 5. g4, and White's pawn majority on the Kingside is just as effective as Black's on the Queenside.

B) 1 . . . g5 2. f4 f6 3. e4 a5. Now, not 4. e5 + ? fxe5 + 5. fxe5 + Ke6 6. Ke4 b4, winning, but 4. h4! and Black is stymied.

After **1. e4?** play continued **1 . . . g5!**(threatening to paralyze White's Kingside with 2 . . . g4) **2. f4 gxf4 3. gxf4 Kc5 4. Kc3 a5 5. Kd3 h5! 6. h4** (or 6. Kc3 b4 + 7. axb4 + axb4 + 8. Kd3 h4 9. h3 b3 10. Kc3 b2 11. Kxb2 Kd4 12. e5 Ke4 13. Kc3 Kxf4 14. Kd4 Kg3 and wins) **6 . . . b4 7. a4 f6! 8. f5**, which warrants its own diagram (following). **Black Won.**
0–1 (54)

WHITE: **Seirawan**   TACTIC: **TRIANGULATION**
BLACK: **Kasparov**
WHERE: **Niksic 1983**

ACTUAL POSITION

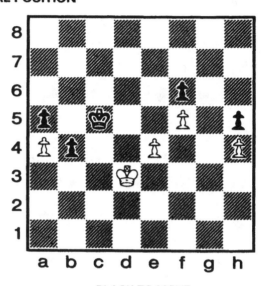

BLACK TO MOVE

ANALYSIS: The right move is **1 . . . Kc6!**. The wrong move is 1 . . . b3?, which discourages victory after 2. Kc3 b2 3. Kxb2 Kd4 4. Kb3 Kxe4 5. Kc4 Kxf5 6. Kb5 Kg4 7. Kxa5 f5 8. Kb4 f4 9. a5 f3 10. a6 f2 11. a7 f1/Q 12. a8/Q.

The game proceeded **2. Kc4 Kc7! 3. Kd3 Kd7!**, and it's *zugzwang*. White can no longer maintain the correspondence of squares. Thus if 4. Kc4, then 4 . . . Kc6; and if 4. Kd4, then 4 . . . Kd6. The end was **4. Ke3 Kc6! 5. Kd3 Kc5 6. Ke3 b3 7. Kd3 Kb4 8. e5 Ka3!**. Black is the first to Queen, releasing a check. **White Resigned.**

0–1 (54)

WHITE: **Kasparov**   TACTIC: OVERLOAD
BLACK: **Gligoric**
WHERE: **Niksic 1983**

ACTUAL POSITION

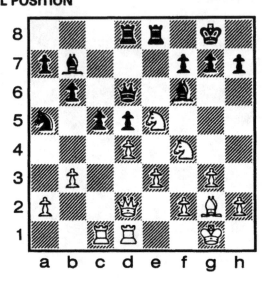

WHITE TO MOVE

ANALYSIS: If White were to play 1. dxc5, it would hang his Knight at e5. Otherwise this capture wins a pawn, for Black's b-pawn must stay to defend his Knight. Kasparov instead resorted to **1. Ng4!**, set up to pilfer the c-pawn. A few possibilities:

A) 1 . . . cxd4 (trying to save the pawn) 2. Nxf6+ Qxf6 3. Qxd4, and no matter how Black plays it, he's going to lose his d-pawn to White's bull's-eyed onslaught.

B) 1 . . . c4. This loses two pieces for a Rook after 2. bxc4 Nxc4 3. Rxc4 dxc4 4. Bxb7. White's ace is that he can always interpose Nxf6+ somewhere along the line.

C) 1 . . . Bg5. It counterattacks on f4, but 2. dxc5 Qd7 3. h3, and White keeps his extra pawn yet provides an escape hatch at h2 for the Knight at g4.

In the game, Gligoric (Black) chose to preserve his dark-square Bishop by **1 . . . Be7**, and gained nothing for his lost pawn after **2. dxc5**. **White Won.**

1–0 (37)

WHITE: **Kasparov**   TACTIC: **MATING ATTACK**
BLACK: **Spassky**
WHERE: **Niksic 1983**
POSSIBLE POSITION

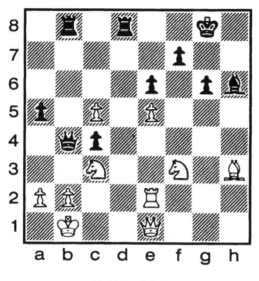

BLACK TO MOVE

ANALYSIS: A superlative lesson in melding a mate, in this case by Spassky rather than Kasparov. Given this opportunity, Black would find **1 . . . Qxc3!**, when 2. Qxc3 is answered by 2 . . . Rd1 + and 3 . . . Rc1 mate. **Black Wins.**
0–1 (33)

WHITE: **Kasparov** TACTIC: **DISCOVERED ATTACK**
BLACK: **Spassky**
WHERE: **Niksic 1983**
POSSIBLE POSITION

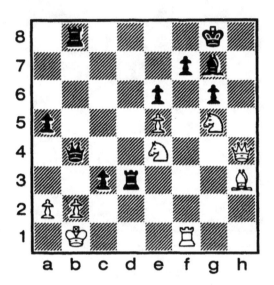

WHITE TO MOVE

ANALYSIS: Black can mate with Qxb2, but it's White on the move. The turnabout move is **1. Nf6+**. If 1 . . . Bxf6, then 2. Qh7+ Kf8 3. Qxf7 is mate. And if 1 . . . Kf8, then 2. Ngh7+ Ke7 3. Nd5++, a double check that snares the Black Queen. **White Wins.**
0–1 (33)

WHITE: **Kasparov**   TACTIC: DOUBLE ATTACK
BLACK: **Korchnoi**
WHERE: **London 1983, Match Game 9**
POSSIBLE POSITION

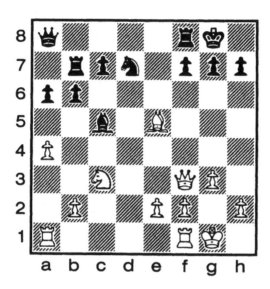

WHITE TO MOVE

ANALYSIS: Black shifted his Knight away from the Bishop's attack (Nf6-d7) and now it boomerangs on the Bishop. Or does it? The winning combination is **1. Bxg7!**, when 1 . . . Kxg7 is dealt with by 2. Qg4 +, forking the King and the hoofless Knight. Thus White wins a pawn as he disrupts Black's Kingside. **White Wins.** 1–0 (32)

WHITE: **Kasparov**   TACTIC: **TRAPPED PIECE**
BLACK: **Korchnoi**
WHERE: London 1983, Match Game 9
ACTUAL POSITION

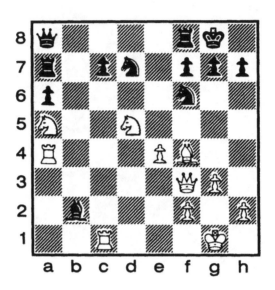

WHITE TO MOVE

ANALYSIS: The Black Rook at a7 is hemmed in. Kasparov divebombs with **1. Ne7 + ! Kh8 2. Rc2**, when Black simply cannot avoid 3. Nec6 winning the exchange. For example:

 A) 2 . . . Nb6 3. Rb4 Ba1 4. Nec6.

 B) 2 . . . Ne5 3. Bxe5 Bxe5 4. Nac6! Qe8 5. Ra5!

In the game Korchnoi tried **2 . . . Qe8**, and the finish was **3. Rxb2 Qxe7 4. Nc6 Qc5 5. Nxa7 Qxa7 6. e5 Ng8 7. Be3 Qa8 8. Qxa8 Rxa8 9. f4 Ne7 10. Rd2!**, and **Black Resigned**, giving Kasparov a 3-1 lead in the semifinal match.
1–0 (32)

WHITE: **Korchnoi**   TACTIC: **MATING ATTACK**
BLACK: **Kasparov**
WHERE: **London 1983, Match Game 10**
POSSIBLE POSITION

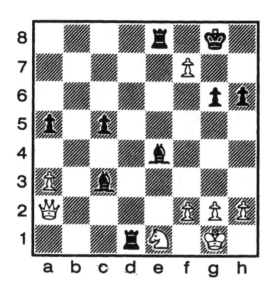

BLACK TO MOVE

ANALYSIS: Another extremely deceptive position. White has a Queen for two Rooks, and Black has two Bishops for a Knight. Advantage Black. But White's f-pawn is forking the enemy King and Rook, so Korchnoi can expect to win some material. Except Kasparov has seen further.

The right lob is **1 . . . Kg7!!**. The move 1 . . . Kh7 fails to 2. Qe2! Red8 3. f8/Q Rxf8 4. Qxd1, giving White the advantage.

After **1 . . . Kg7!!**, play goes **2. fxe8/N + Kf8 3. h4** (3. f4 Bd4 + 4. Kf1 Bd3 + wins) **3 . . . Rxe1 + 4. Kh2 Be5 + 5. Kh3** (5. g3 permits 5 . . . Rh1 mate) **5 . . . Bf5 + 6. g4 Be4**, and there's no satisfactory stand-off to 7 . . . Rh1 mate. White would have to cede his Queen. **Black Wins.**
Draw (42)

WHITE: **Korchnoi**   TACTIC: **MATING ATTACK**
BLACK: **Kasparov**
WHERE: **London 1983, Match Game 10**
POSSIBLE POSITION

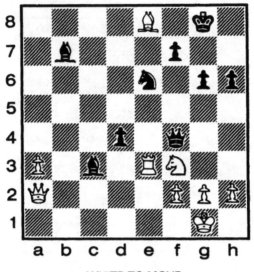

WHITE TO MOVE

ANALYSIS: Black is down the exchange, though his menacing passed d-pawn might force White into concessions. But it's White's move, and a sudden sacrifice undermines Black's game: **1. Bxf7 + !**. If 1 . . . Qxf7, then 2. Rxe6, followed by 3. Ne5, pounds away at Black's bastions. Meanwhile, 1 . . . Kxf7 is hopeless after 2. Qxe6 +. So Black plays **1 . . . Kf8**, which leads to **2. Rxe6 Qc1 + 3. Ne1 Bxe1 4. Re8 + Kg7 5. Rg8 + Kf6** (5 . . . Kh7 6. Bxg6 mate) **6. Rxg6 +**, and White's Queen barges in to coordinate the mating checks. **White Wins.**
Draw (42)

WHITE: **Kasparov**   TACTIC: **PASSED PAWN**
BLACK: **Korchnoi**
WHERE: **London 1983, Match Game 11**
ACTUAL POSITION

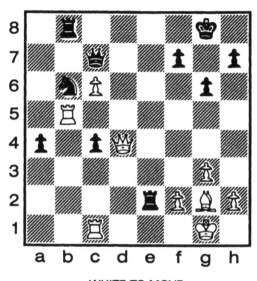

WHITE TO MOVE

ANALYSIS: Black's passed Queenside pawns, now split and supported by a wobbly Knight, prove no match for White's pushy c-pawn and diligent Bishop. Kasparov began his final push with **1. Bf3!**, providing his King a hole at g2 while forcing Black's Rook into a declaration. Black's Rook withdrew all the way with **1 . . . Re8**.

This proved correct. After a random retreat, say 1 . . . Re6, Kasparov had intended 2. Rcb1. Play might then go 2 . . . a3 (there's really nothing better) 3. Rxb6 Rxb6 4. Qxb6 a2 (5. Qxc7 is now met by 5 . . . axb1/Q+) 5. Qb8+! Qxb8 (or 5 . . . Kg7 6. Qb2+ followed by 7. Qxa2) 6. Rxb8+ Kg7 7. Ra8 Re1+ 8. Kg2 (the importance of **1. Bf3!** is instantly clear; if White's Bishop were still at g2, White would face a mucky situation after blocking by Bf1) 8 . . . a1/Q 9. Rxa1 Rxa1 10. c7, and White crowns a new Queen.

White actually continued **2. Qc5!**. This rebuffs the advance 2 . . . a3 and lays the carpet for 3. Rcb1. The immediate 2. Rcb1 bumps into difficulties after 2 . . . a3 3. Rxb6 Rxb6 4. Qxb6 a2 because White can't check on b8 with his Queen, as in the previous note.

After **2. Qc5!**, Korchnoi, running out of viable moves, tried **2 . . . Qe7**. But after **3. c7 Qxc5 4. Rxc5 Rbc8 5. Bb7 Nd7 6. R5xc4,** the most famous of defecting Soviet chess masters had to relent. **Black Resigned.** This victory made Kasparov a semifinalist in the quest for the world championship title.

1–0 (32)

7

KARPOV: THE FIRST ROUND

And so it was on to Vilnius in March 1984 and the finals match with Vassily Smyslov—a battle of youth versus age, for in March Smyslov would celebrate his sixty-third birthday. A formidable figure in the chess world since the 1940s, Smyslov toppled the mighty Botvinnik from his throne in 1957. The days when Smyslov could successfully compete for the title were thought to be long gone, and yet here he was, only two steps away from the crown that he once wore. Would there be a Cinderella denouement for the grand old man?

The final score was four wins for Kasparov to none for Smyslov, but in truth Smyslov played no less strongly than he had in earlier matches where he defeated Hübner and Ribli. Kasparov was simply too strong for him. And the fact that there were no losses was important, for the match with Karpov in September would be played to six victories, or six defeats, with draws not counting.

But before this match occurred a bit of friendly rivalry took place: the USSR versus the World, a match over ten boards, with the players meeting each other four times. Kasparov on board number two prevailed over Timman, drawing the first three games and winning the fourth.

A full description of the first match with Karpov for the world championship would fill at least one entire book on its own, but here are a few highlights. Perhaps underestimating his opponent (if that is possible), Kasparov got off to a dreadful start, losing four of the first nine games and winning none. But once he dug in his heels, no less than seventeen consecutive draws followed. This was indeed a record, but then all sorts of records were broken during this marathon contest.

The match had seemed as good as over when at last Karpov broke through to win game number 27. But here the psychological roles were reversed. Kasparov, having done all that could be reasonably expected after his terrible start, relaxed, for surely the end was inevitable. The pressure was on Karpov to put away the sixth victory that would end the match. Karpov certainly had the opportunities, but the length of the trial was taking its toll and somehow he could not quite summon up the energy to totally dispose of Kasparov. And thus the match went on.

In the 32nd game, the challenger began to score. Fourteen draws followed, and then suddenly the champion collapsed, dropping games number 47 and 48. Karpov's game was unrecognizable. It was now February 9, exactly five months since the match began.

On Sunday, February 10, Florencio Campomanes, FIDE president, flew to Moscow. Two unscheduled time-outs were called and then on Friday, February 15, Campomanes announced at a press conference "that the match is ended without decision. A new match shall be played from scratch, starting September 1985." The audience was stunned, and in the midst of all the buzzing, Karpov and Kasparov both approached the podium to render their objections.

The match regulations clearly empowered the FIDE president to make such sweeping decisions, but Campomanes certainly realized at the time that his edict needed some bolstering. Taking the two parties behind closed doors, he obtained their reluctant consent and emerged one hour later to confirm that his initial decision would take effect. A new match would be played.

WHITE: Smyslov   TACTIC: REMOVING THE GUARD
BLACK: Kasparov
WHERE: Vilnius 1984
POSSIBLE POSITION

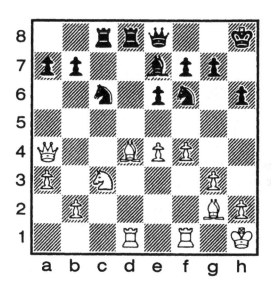

BLACK TO MOVE

ANALYSIS: White's Bishop seems adequately protected, but a mini disruption can alter the situation. Here Black wins a piece with **1 . . . b5!**, for 2. Nxb5 Nxd4 3. Rxd4 Rxd4 4. Qxd4 fails to 4 . . . Qxb5. **Black Wins.**
Draw (41)

WHITE: **Smyslov**   TACTIC: **REMOVING THE GUARD**
BLACK: **Kasparov**
WHERE: **Vilnius 1984**
POSSIBLE POSITION

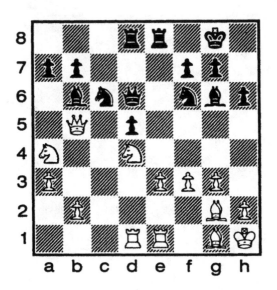

BLACK TO MOVE

ANALYSIS: White has just played Nc3-a4 to exchange a Knight for a Bishop, a situation fraught with dangerous consequences. Black dominates with **1 . . . Bxd4 2. exd4 Bc2 3. Rxe8 + Nxe8! 4. Rc1 a6** (distracting the Queen from the Knight's defense) **5. Qxb7 Bxa4 6. b3 Rb8 7. Qxa6 Bb5** and White must lose even more material. On 8. Rxc6 Bxa6 9. Rxd6 Nxd6, Black emerges a Rook ahead, thanks to **3 . . . Nxe8!**. **Black Wins.**
Draw (41)

WHITE: **Kasparov** TACTIC: **DOUBLE ATTACK**
BLACK: **Smyslov**
WHERE: **Vilnius 1984**
POSSIBLE POSITION

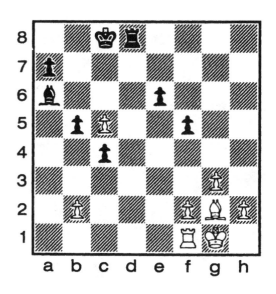

WHITE TO MOVE

ANALYSIS: Black's last move (Rh8-d8) relegates his Rook to an ineffectual position. White can seize his chance with **1. Ra1!**. If 1 . . . Bb7, then 2. c6 Ba8 3. c7! wins a piece. Capturing the c-pawn (3 . . . Kxc7) loses the Bishop by 4. Rxa7 + and 5. Rxa8. **White Wins.**
Draw (36)

WHITE: **Smyslov**   TACTIC: PIN
BLACK: **Kasparov**
WHERE: **Vilnius 1984**
POSSIBLE POSITION

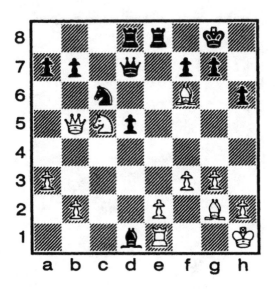

BLACK TO MOVE

ANALYSIS: Black is an exchange ahead, but with the Queen, Rook and Bishop attacked, how long can he keep the money in the bank? Time for the Lone Ranger to show, and the surprising desperado tactic is **1 . . . Bxe2!!**, when **2. Rxe2 Qf5** (threatening 3 . . . Qb1 +) **3. Rxe8 + Rxe8 4. Bc3 d4! 5. Bd2 b6!**, which leads to the win of the pinned Knight. A bad continuation would be 6. Qxc6, for 6 . . . Qb1 + mates now that White's Queen has ceded control of f1. **Black Wins.**
Draw (28)

WHITE: **Smyslov**   TACTIC: **REMOVING THE GUARD**
BLACK: **Kasparov**
WHERE: **Vilnius 1984**
POSSIBLE POSITION

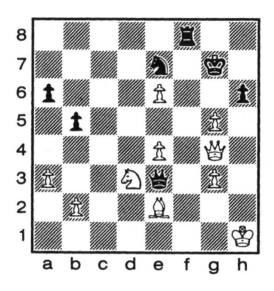

BLACK TO MOVE

ANALYSIS: White has lost a Rook for a Bishop, but is compensated by three extra pawns. His position, however, is flimsily strung together by the Bishop at e2, protected by the Queen at g4. It all unravels after **1 . . . h5!**, which wins Black the Bishop. Either White must lose his Queen (2. Qxh5 Rh8, pinning it to the King) or abandon the Bishop by moving off the e2-h5 diagonal. Black winds up a Rook ahead with mate in the offing. **Black Wins.** 0–1 (40)

WHITE: **Smyslov**   TACTIC: **ZUGZWANG**
BLACK: **Kasparov**
WHERE: **Vilnius 1984**

ACTUAL POSITION

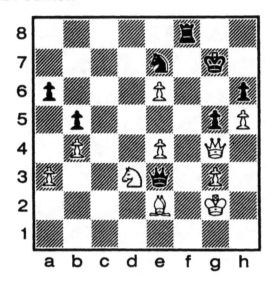

BLACK TO MOVE

ANALYSIS: With two pawns for the exchange, White seems in reasonable shape. Nevertheless, **1 . . . Kh7** promulgates a *zugzwang*! None of White's pieces may move:

A) The Queen must attend to defense of the Bishop.

B) The Bishop must guard the Knight (if 1. Bf1, then 1 . . . Rxf1 2. Kxf1 Qxd3 +).

C) The Knight must maintain control over f2 to prevent a Rook invasion.

What's left are King and pawn moves. So **2. Kh2** (2 e5 Kh8 changes nothing) **2 . . . Rd8** (this is now possible because White now cannot safely retreat his Knight to f2) **3. e5 Rxd3 4. Bxd3 Qxd3. White Resigned.** This victory in game 12 of the match gave Kasparov a lead of four games. When the 13th and last game was a draw, Kasparov became the official challenger to Karpov's crown.

0–1 (40)

WHITE: Kasparov
BLACK: Timman
WHERE: London 1984
POSSIBLE POSITION

TACTIC: **HAND-TO-HAND
FIGHTING**

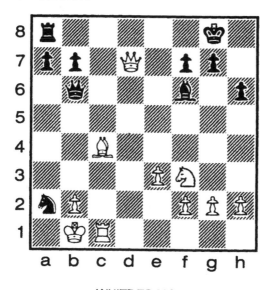

WHITE TO MOVE

ANALYSIS: White is menaced with mate at b2. How to go? One could instinctively lash out with 1. Bxf7 +, then 1 . . . Kf8 (1 . . . Kh7 2. Qf5 + Kh8 3. Rc8 + Rxc8 4. Qxc8 + is hopeless. Black either gets mated by 4 . . . Kh7 5. Qg8 or loses the Knight at a2 after 4 . . . Qd8 [or 4 . . . Bd8] 5. Qxd8 + Bxd8 6. Kxa2) 2. Nd4 (not 2. Rc2 Nc3 + 3. Kc1 Rd8) 2 . . . Bxd4 (no time for 2 . . . Nxc1 as White insinuates 3. Ne6 +) 3. exd4 Rd8! (even here 3 . . . Nxc1 is bad because of 4. Be6!) 4. Rc8 Rxc8 5. Qxc8 + (can't toy with 5. Bxa2 as 5 . . . Qg6 + turns the tables) 5 . . . Kxf7 6. Qc4 +, followed by taking the Knight at a2. This line leads to a drawish position.

Much stronger than 1. Bxf7 + for Kasparov is the quiet **1. Rc2!**, leading to an intricate line of play:

1 . . . Rd8 (1 . . . Nc3 + 2. Kc1 Ne4 3. Bxf7 + Kh8 4. Ne5!— much stronger than 4. Rc8 + Rxc8 5. Qxc8 Qd8—4 . . . Rd8 5.

Ng6+ Kh7 6. Qf5 and Black is helpless against the impending Nf8+ and Qh7 mate).

So **2. Qxf7+ Kh7 3. Kxa2 Qa5+ 4. Kb1 Rd1+ 5. Rc1 Qf5+** (5 . . . Rxc1+ 6. Kxc1 Qa1+ 7. Kd2 Qxb2+ 8. Kd1 Qb1+ 9. Ke2 Qb2+ 10. Nd2 and White is safe), and White has the vital deflection **6. e4** (otherwise 6. Ka2 Qa5+ repeats the position). After **6 . . . Qxe4+ 7. Ka2 Rxc1 8. Qg8+ Kg6 9. Bf7+ Kf5 10. Qh7+ Kf4 11. g3+ Kxf3 12. Bh5+**, White procures the Queen. **White Wins.**

1–0 (34)

WHITE: Kasparov   TACTIC: DOUBLE ATTACK
BLACK: Timman
WHERE: London 1984
POSSIBLE POSITION

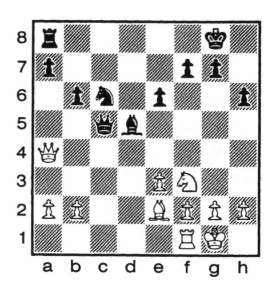

WHITE TO MOVE

ANALYSIS: The right line wins White a piece, starting with **1. e4**. Black could respond **1 . . . b5**, trying to dislodge the Queen from the defense of e4. But after **2. Bxb5 Bxe4 3. Qxe4 Qxb5**, White snares a piece by **4. Nd4**, which forks the Queen and Knight. Black cannot play 4 . . . Nxd4 because of 5. Qxa8 +. **White Wins.** Draw (24)

WHITE: **Kasparov**   TACTIC: **DOUBLE ATTACK**
BLACK: **Timman**
WHERE: **London 1984**
POSSIBLE POSITION

WHITE TO MOVE

ANALYSIS: White's Queen, ensconced in the Black camp, aims at Black's Knight, defended by the Bishop at a4. Divert the Bishop is the initial theme. White should play **1. Bd1!**, a powerful and surprising retreat that recalls Kasparov-Gligoric at Niksic 1983 (see page 126). A few of Black's defenses:

A) 1 . . . Bxd1 2. Qxd7 Rc1 3. Nb3!, exploiting the pin on the Bishop to the Rook along the first rank while uncovering the d-file for the Queen. White acquires material.

B) 1 . . . Bb5 2. Nxb5 Qxb5 3. Ba4, skewering the Knight at d7.

C) **1 . . . Nc5** (best) **2. Bxa4 Qxa4** (2 . . . Nxa4? 3. Nc6 followed by 4. Ne7 +—if 3 . . . Rxc6 in this line, then 4. Qa8 + wins the exchange) **3. Qxb6** takes a pawn, for if 3 . . . Qxa2, then 4. Nc6 picks up even more. **White Wins.**
Draw (24)

WHITE: **Karpov**   TACTIC: **VULNERABLE BACK RANK**
BLACK: **Kasparov**
WHERE: **Moscow 1984-85, Match Game 3**
ACTUAL POSITION

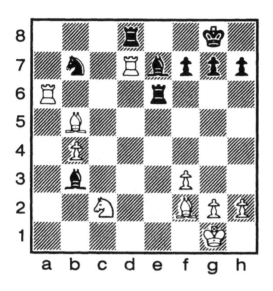

WHITE TO MOVE

ANALYSIS: Black is down a pawn and his pieces are all tangled. The Knight at b7 is particularly vulnerable. Karpov continued **1. Rxe6** (removing the guard for the Bishop at e7) **1 . . . Rxd7** (on 1 . . . fxe6 2. Rxe7 Bxc2 3. Rxe6—3. Rxb7 allows 3 . . . Rd1 + — White is a sound two pawns up) **2. Re1** (securing the back rank and maintaining his threat to Black's Rook) **2 . . . Rc7 3. Bb6** and **Black Resigned**. If 3 . . . Rxc2, then 4. Rxe7 Nd6 5. Bc5 wins the Knight. If it moves, then 6. Re8 is mate. And if Black protects it by 5 . . . Rd2, then 6. Bxd6 threatens mate and deters Black from taking back his piece. A terrible loss for Kasparov, and it gave Karpov the first lead in the match.
1–0 (31)

WHITE: **Kasparov**   TACTIC: **PIN**
BLACK: **Karpov**
WHERE: **Moscow 1984-85, Match Game 6**
POSSIBLE POSITION

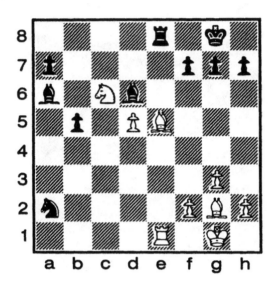

WHITE TO MOVE

ANALYSIS: Who is pinning who? For now, White's Bishop is pinned to his Rook by Black's Rook. After **1. Ra1**, the pin slips to the other foot. Black therefore tries **1 . . . Bxe5**, which leads to **2. Rxa2 Bc8 3. Re2** (here we go again) **3 . . . f6 4. f4 Bg4 5. Re4** (5. Re1 or 5. Re3 allows 5 . . . Bd4) **5 . . . Bf5 6. fxe5 Bxe4 7. Bxe4**, followed by advancing White's passed pawn (d6-d7).

After **1. Ra1 Bxe5 2. Rxa2**, Black needn't play **2 . . . Bc8**, but could essay 2 . . . Bb7. Nonetheless, the passed pawn still succeeds after 3. Rxa7 Bxc6 4. dxc6. Although the passed pawn has switched files, it remains a powerhouse. The line concludes: 4 . . . Kf8 5. Bh3! Re7 6. Bd7, threatening both c7 and Ra8 + .
White Wins.
0–1 (70)

WHITE: **Karpov**   TACTIC: **SKEWER**
BLACK: **Kasparov**
WHERE: **Moscow 1984-85, Match Game 15**
POSSIBLE POSITION

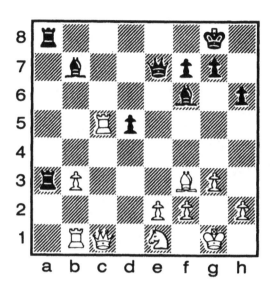

BLACK TO MOVE

ANALYSIS: White's overworked Queen is guarding too many soldiers. After **1 . . . Ra1** (threatening 2 . . . Rxb1 and 3 . . . Qxc5), White is in a pickle. If 2. Rxa1, then 2 . . . Rxa1 3. Qc2 Rxe1+ wins a piece. And if 2. Rc7 instead, then 2 . . . Rxb1 3. Rxe7 Rxc1, and Black clearly comes out top dog. **Black Wins.**
Draw (93)

WHITE: **Karpov**   TACTIC: **OVERLOAD**
BLACK: **Kasparov**
WHERE: **Moscow 1984-85, Match Game 27**
ACTUAL POSITION

WHITE TO MOVE

ANALYSIS: It's a tense struggle, with both sides on the verge of Queening. Black's difficulty is that his Rook has to guard his pawn and stop the c-pawn from promoting. The problem magnifies after **1. Re2**, forking the Bishop and pawn. If Black saves his Bishop, say 1 . . . Bb3, then White merely grabs the h-pawn, 2. Rxh2. Black cannot capitalize on a capture of White's Rook because the c-pawn then promotes. Thus **Black Resigned** after **1. Re2**.

This was Karpov's last victory in the match. In the remaining 21 games he scored 18 draws and 3 losses. The final victory (Karpov already had 5 of the 6 wins he needed at this point) somehow eluded him, a magnificent testimony to Kasparov's sangfroid. The stripling contender played the last 21 games with the wolf at the door and lived to become the leader of the pack.
1-0 (59)

WHITE: **Kasparov**   TACTIC: **DOUBLE CHECK**
BLACK: **Karpov**
WHERE: **Moscow 1984-85, Match Game 46**
POSSIBLE POSITION

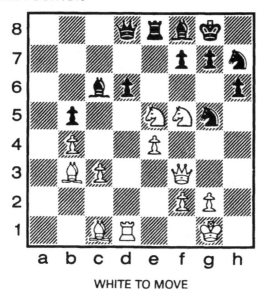

WHITE TO MOVE

ANALYSIS: A twofold purpose, a twofold failure. Black pirouetted his Knight to g5 to defend f7 and to gain time by attacking White's Queen. But something terrible happens. There's an explosion with **1. Bxf7 +**, when 1 . . . Kh8 is greeted by 2. Ng6 mate. And after the more likely **1 . . . Nxf7**, the sky falls with **2. Nxf7 Kxf7 3. Nxh6 + +** and **4. Qf7** mate, no matter how Black answers. **White Wins.**
Draw (41)

WHITE: **Kasparov** TACTIC: **DISCOVERED ATTACK**
BLACK: **Karpov**
WHERE: **Moscow 1984-85, Match Game 46**
POSSIBLE POSITION

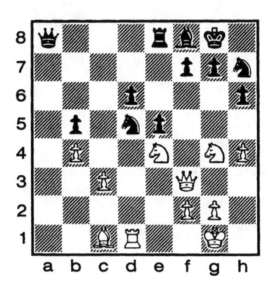

WHITE TO MOVE

ANALYSIS: For now, Black's Knight at d5 seems guarded, but White's sword is still in its scabbard. When he flashes it forth with **1. Rxd5,** Black must perceive that **1 . . . Qxd5** encounters **2. Ne-f6+ Nxf6 3. Nxf6+**, winning the Black Queen. **White Wins.** Draw (41)

WHITE: **Karpov**   TACTIC: **KNIGHT FORK**
BLACK: **Kasparov**
WHERE: **Moscow 1984-85, Match Game 47**
ACTUAL POSITION

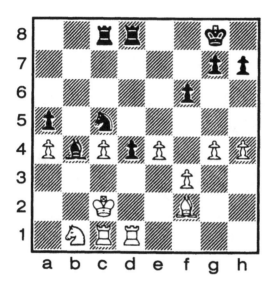

BLACK TO MOVE

ANALYSIS: White is currently up a pawn, yet Black's orchestrated pieces and surging d-pawn mean harmony. Kasparov's coda was **1 . . . d3+ 2. Kb2 d2.** After the obligatory **3. Rc2,** Black curtain-calls the Bishop with the Knight fork **3 . . . Nd3+.** White can do no better than to sacrifice the exchange. **White Resigned.** This was the shortest game Karpov had lost as world champion, a title he held for ten years.
0–1 (32)

WHITE: **Kasparov**   TACTIC: **DISCOVERED CHECK**
BLACK: **Karpov**
WHERE: **Moscow 1984-85, Match Game 48**
POSSIBLE POSITION

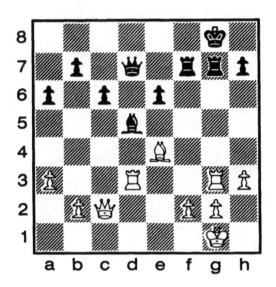

WHITE TO MOVE

ANALYSIS: Material is even, White has the move, and haunches up a veiled attack. Here he can win a pawn by **1. Bxh7 + !**. If Black takes the Bishop (1 . . . Kxh7, for the Rook is pinned), then **2. Rxd5 +** discovers a deadly check and secures the Black Queen. **White Wins.**

WHITE: **Kasparov** TACTIC: **IN-BETWEEN CHECK**
BLACK: **Karpov**
WHERE: **Moscow 1984-85, Match Game 48**
ACTUAL POSITION

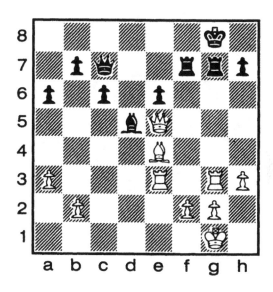

WHITE TO MOVE

ANALYSIS: White's centralized pieces against Black's deficient pawns and squares tell the story. Kasparov pinched a pawn with **1. Rxg7 +**. This exchange lures Black's Rook off the f-file. After **1 . . . Rxg7**, White continued **2. Bxd5**. If Black retorts 2 . . . cxd5, his e-pawn goes down with check. If the e-pawn takes the Bishop instead (2 . . . exd5), then 3. Qe8 is mate. So Black first opted for White's Queen with **2 . . . Qxe5**, and White preempted a pawn with **3. Bxe6 + Qxe6 4. Rxe6. White Won.**
1–0 (67)

8

WORLD
CHAMPION

Of course, the chess world was in turmoil after the great
match. Over the next several months each of the three partici-
pants, plus chief juryman Alfred Kinzel and chief arbiter Gligoric,
all had their say. Comments were made about everything from
the Campomanes decision itself (many observers feel it was
marked by a bias in favor of Karpov), to the obvious behind-
scenes maneuvering that led up to it. Kasparov, who in May and
June played training matches with Hübner in Hamburg and Andersson in Belgrade, took these opportunities to grant some
rather frank interviews to the press, the kind rarely heard from
prominent non-defected Soviet figures. In these interviews Kasparov severely criticized both Campomanes and the Soviet Chess
Federation. It appears that Kasparov, having recovered himself in
the match, was the only party who wanted the match continued
without interruption, but his views were ignored. Quite naturally
he felt bitter about the whole episode.

The controversy surrounding the match in Moscow will not escape discussion by the chess world at large for years to come. Unfortunately, it is difficult to divide the personalities involved from the issues that have been raised. However, it is not the purpose of this book to judge any aspect of this matter.

On the other hand, perhaps this match will at least lay to rest the specter of unlimited matches in the future. The contest for the world championship is one that should be primarily a test of skill. Sporting attitude and stamina, though important, should play a lesser part.

The second match in Moscow got under way in early September as scheduled. When, on November 9, the 24th and last game concluded, its progress could be described as more or less normal for a world championship match. The contestants were of approximately equal strength, but at the very end it was Kasparov who held a two-point edge. Thus the title passed to the hands of the very capable thirteenth champion of the world. May this be a lucky thirteenth, both for Kasparov and for the chess world.

WHITE: Kasparov   TACTIC: **MATING ATTACK**
BLACK: Hübner
WHERE: Hamburg 1985, Match Game 2
ACTUAL POSITION

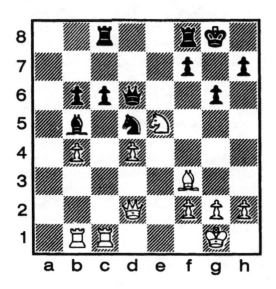

WHITE TO MOVE

ANALYSIS: Many chessplayers have recognized a striking simi-
larity between Kasparov and the once world champion Alexander
Alekhine, particularly in their imaginative style of attack. One
cannot help but remember Spielmann's comments about
Alekhine: "I can see the final combinations as well as Alekhine,
but how he obtains such positions is beyond me." They apply as
well to Kasparov.
   Let's pick up a Kasparov attack in the early stages. It starts with
a pawn advance, **1. h4!**. With **1 . . . Rfd8 2. h5 Ne7 3. Re1!**, White
begins to shift his attacking units to the Kingside. If Black should
take the d-pawn, 3 . . . Qxd4, then 4. Qg5! is hard to counter. For
example, 4 . . . Nf5 (hoping for 5. Rbd1 Qh4!) 5. Bxc6 h6 6. Qf6

and White threatens 7. Qxf7 + followed by 8. Nxg6 mate, as well as 7. Bxb5, winning a piece. Black can doubtless improve his own play, but White still builds an impressive attack.

So Black doesn't play Qxd4 but **3 . . . Rc7**, and White spins out the far-reaching **4. Bg4!**. It dissuades Black from moving his Knight to f5, while clearing the third rank for a Rook lift from b1 to b3 to the Kingside.

Since taking White's d-pawn by Qxd4 is risky, Black recentralizes his Knight with **4 . . . Nd5**. Comes a clearing exchange **5. hxg6 hxg6**, and then a Rook maneuver **6. Rb3**, threatening 7. Rh3 and 8. Qh6.

Back on his heels, Black opens his second rank for defense or escape by **6 . . . f5**. Now the Rook at c7 may be able to shield the King. Unfortunately, 6 . . . f5 weakens the pawn skeleton around Black's King, augmenting White's chances.

White continues **7. Bd1!**, an effective retreat. In the event of 7 . . . Rh7 8. Rg3 Ne7, the Bishop thrusts back into the game by 9. Bb3 +. So instead of 7 . . . Rh7, Black issues **7 . . . Rg7**, which leads to **8. Rh3! Qxb4**. Though down a pawn, White is in better shape (see next diagram).

1–0 (39)

WHITE: **Kasparov**   TACTIC: **MATING ATTACK**
BLACK: **Hübner**
WHERE: **Hamburg 1985, Match Game 2**
ACTUAL POSITION

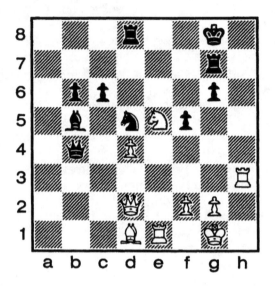

WHITE TO MOVE

Black finally has a pawn, but White has **9. Qh6!!**, abandoning his Rook at e1. Black takes the Rook with check **9 . . . Qxe1+ 10. Kh2**, but then has to make tracks with **10 . . . Kf8**. After **11. Nxg6+ Kg8** (or 11 . . . Kf7 12. Ne5+ Kf8 13. Rg3) **12. Qh8+ Kf7 13. Qxd8, Black Resigned**. There's really no hope. If Black slaps the Bishop with 13 . . . Qxd1, White's Knight reigns: 14. Ne5+ Ke6 15. Rh6+. And if Black takes the Knight instead with 13 . . . Rxg6, White's Bishop takes charge (note: 13 . . . Kxg6 14. Bh5+ followed by 15. Bf7 mate): 14. Rh7+ Rg7 (14 . . . Ke6 15. Qe8+ skewers the Queen) 15. Bh5+ Ke6 16. Rxg7. An exemplary Kasparov-powered attack.
1–0 (39)

WHITE: **Kasparov** TACTIC: **KNIGHT FORK**
BLACK: **Andersson**
WHERE: **Belgrade 1985, Match Game 3**
POSSIBLE POSITION

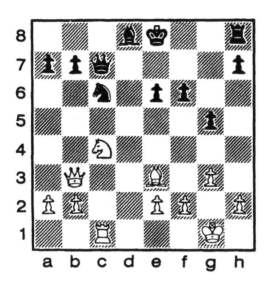

WHITE TO MOVE

ANALYSIS: Black's Queen hovers over his weak points (b7 and d6 for example), but is not immune to an incisive incision. White should play **1. Qxb7!**, diverting Black's Queen to a feckless square while winning a pawn. If Black plays 1 . . . Qxb7, then 2. Nd6+ wins Black's Queen. Otherwise, Black's game disintegrates. **White Wins.**
1–0 (40)

WHITE: **Kasparov**   TACTIC: **DESPERADO**
BLACK: **Andersson**
WHERE: **Belgrade 1985, Match Game 5**
POSSIBLE POSITION

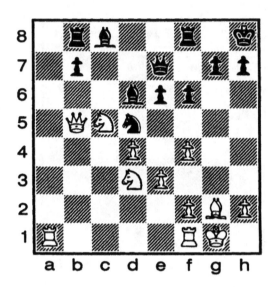

BLACK TO MOVE

ANALYSIS: It's a most difficult moment in any game when a player attempts to unjam his cramped position. Here, instead of 1 . . . Rfd8 (as played by Andersson), allowing the strong counter 2. Ra7, Black might have considered **1 . . . b6**, to force away the annoying Knight at c5. To this Kasparov undoubtedly would have retaliated with **2. Nxe6!**, anticipating the strongest response, the desperado 2 . . . Nxe3. This Black answer is better than 2 . . . Nc3 because of 3. Qb2. After **2 . . . Nxe3**, it's tempting to continue these waltzing tactics with **3. Nxf8 Nxf1**, when White has the muscular maneuver **4. Re1!**. White stands better (see next diagram).
1–0 (50)

WHITE: **Kasparov** TACTIC: **TRAPPED PIECE**
BLACK: **Andersson**
WHERE: **Belgrade 1985, Game 5**
POSSIBLE POSITION

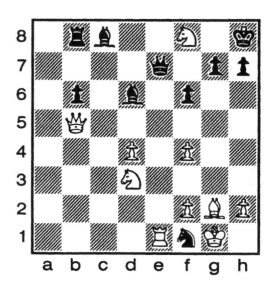

BLACK TO MOVE

ANALYSIS: Since 4 . . . Qxf8 is guillotined by 5. Re8, pinning the plunderer, Black should answer **4 . . . Qf7**. A pregnant discovery could then be formulated by **5. Qe8!** (threat: to move the Knight). If Black then takes the Knight, 5 . . . Qxf8, trouble is manifested with 6. Qxf8 Bxf8 7. Re8 g6 8. Rxf8+ Kg7 9. Rd8 Nd2 10. Bc6 followed by 11. Bd7.

So Black footsies **5 . . . Qg8** (to block the discovery), resulting in **6. Bd5 Bf5** (6 . . . Be6 7. Qxe6 wins). Other moves by the Bishop at c8 are answered similarly to what follows: **7. Qxb8 Bxb8 8. Bxg8 Kxg8 9. Nd7 Bxd7 10. Kxf1 Bb5 11. Ke2 Bxf4 12. Rb1 Bxd3+ 13. Kxd3 Bxh2 14. Rxb6**, giving White every prospect of winning.

Attractive as this line is, it won't work if Black has a serious improvement. Instead of **3 . . . Nxf1** (see previous diagram), Black can test **3 . . . Nxg2.** In that case, 4. Rae1 would be an error: 4 . . . Nxe1 5. Rxe1 Ba6! and the back rank is covered. Probably best is **4. Kxg2** (in response to 3 . . . Nxg2), but after **4 . . . Bb7+,** followed by capturing the Knight on f8, Black has good practical chances. The Bishops' possibilities can expand with White's King being so denuded.

What does all this signify? That White must play the pedestrian **3. fxe3!** if he hopes to derive advantage. Then after **3 . . . Bxe6 4. e4,** White still retains a spatial superiority.

1–0 (50)

WHITE: **Kasparov**   TACTIC: **VULNERABLE BACK RANK**
BLACK: **Andersson**
WHERE: **Belgrade 1985, Match Game 5**
POSSIBLE POSITION

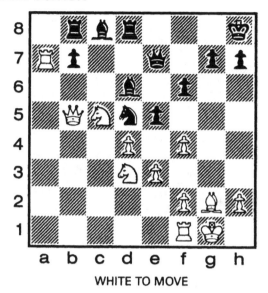

WHITE TO MOVE

ANALYSIS: If Andersson makes a bid for freedom with . . . e5? Kasparov is ready: **1. fxe5** (1. Bxd5 Bxc5 and Black regains the piece with 2 . . . Rxd5) **1 . . . fxe5 2. dxe5 Bxe5 3. Nxe5 Qxe5 4. Rd1 Bg4.**
   White now seemingly abandons his Rook and plays **5. Nxb7!!**. If 5 . . . Bxd1, then 6. Nxd8 Rxb5 (or 6 . . . Rxd8 7. Qxd5) 7. Nf7 + Kg8 8. Nxe5 concludes with White a clear pawn ahead. But in answer to **5. Nxb7!!** Black abracadabras **5 . . . Nxe3!**. The euphoria, however, is tempered by **6. Rxd8 + Rxd8 7. Ra8!!** (naturally, not 7. Qxe5 because of 7 . . . Rd1 + and 8. Rxf1 mate). Now if 7 . . . Rxa8, White can safely annex the Queen (8. Qxe5) since a1 is then guarded by White's Queen. So Black must try **7 . . . Bc8!**, which eventually loses to **8. Qe2! Qg5 9. fxe3 Bxb7 10. Rxd8 + Qxd8 11. Bxb7**. And this is just off the top of Gary Kasparov's head. **White Wins.**
1–0 (50)

WHITE: **Kasparov**   TACTIC: **PASSED PAWN**
BLACK: **Andersson**
WHERE: **Belgrade 1985, Match Game 5**
POSSIBLE POSITION

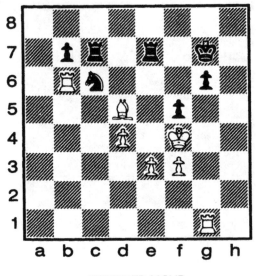

WHITE TO MOVE

ANALYSIS: The position in the diagram was reached on Kasparov's analysis board while the game was adjourned. Playing for *zugzwang*, the proposal was **1. Rg2!**. Black might then reply 1 . . . Re8. So What else could he try? The Knight at c6 must stand rigid because of 2. Rxg6, and the Rook at c7 is stapled to the defense of c6. If 1 . . . Red7, then 2. Be6 and 3. Bxf5 decides. Meanwhile, 1 . . . Kf6 meets with 2. Bb3, and the advance of the d-pawn should conjure a win.

But after **1 . . . Re8**, White could still snake around with **2. Bb3!** Black might try counterattacking on e3 with **2 . . . Rce7** (blunderous is 2 . . . Rd7 3. d5 Ne5 4. Ba4, gaining the exchange), but this fails to **3. d5 Ne5** (g6 must be protected) **4. d6 Nd3+ 5. Kg5 Rxe3 6. Rxb7+ Kf8 7. Rh7**, when White has deadly alternatives such as Kh6, Kf6 and Rh8. White should win.
1–0 (50)

WHITE: **Kasparov**   TACTIC: **MATING ATTACK**
BLACK: **Andersson**
WHERE: **Belgrade 1985, Match Game 5**
POSSIBLE POSITION

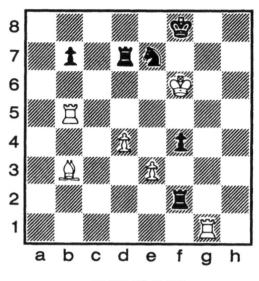

WHITE TO MOVE

ANALYSIS: White's pieces must stab a few times to get at the Black King: **1. Rh5!** (merely threatens mate) **1 . . . Rd6+** (1 . . . fxe3+ means zero after 2. Ke6, salivating over 3. Rh8+ and 3. Kxd7) **2. Be6 fxe3+ 3. Ke5** with victory next door. **White Wins.** 1–0 (50)

WHITE: **Kasparov**   TACTIC: **PASSED PAWN**
BLACK: **Andersson**
WHERE: **Belgrade 1985, Match Game 5**
POSSIBLE POSITION

WHITE TO MOVE

ANALYSIS: All else being equal, Black's last move (f2) knocks at the door of new Queendom. A stop order on this changeling is for White to play **1. Bc4**, perhaps persuading Black to resign.

For example:

A) 1 . . . Rc2 2. Ra5! Rxc4 3. Ra8 + Nd8 4. Rxd8 + Rxd8 5. e7 + Ke8 6. Rg8 + Kd7 7. exd/Q + , and White will catch the f-pawn by 8. Qe8 + and 9. Qe2, among other things.

B) 1 . . . f1/Q + 2. Bxf1 Rf2 + 3. Rf5 Rxf5 4. Kxf5 Rxd4 5. Rf6 (not 5. exf7 Kxf7 with a drawish ending), and White wins the pinned Knight while retaining his last pawn.

C) 1 . . . Rxb5 2. Bxb5 Rc7 3. Rg2 (not 3. exf7 Rxf7 + and the subsequent 4 . . . f1/Q) 3 . . . Nd6 4. Bd3 Rc3 5. e7 + Ke8 6. Bb5 + ! Rc6 (if 6 . . . Nxb5 then 7. Rg8 + Kd7 8. e8 (Q) +) 7. Bxc6 + bxc6 8. Ke6!, which certifies the mate. **White Wins.**
1–0 (50)

WHITE: **Kasparov**   TACTIC: IN-BETWEEN CHECK
BLACK: **Andersson**
WHERE: **Belgrade 1985, Match Game 5**
POSSIBLE POSITION

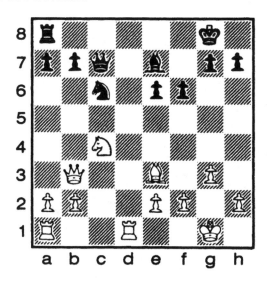

WHITE TO MOVE

ANALYSIS: The position is balanced, but Black has potential targets at b7 and e6. Bells can ring with **1. Nd6!**, threatening the e- and b-pawns. If Black taps the Knight with 1 . . . Bxd6, then 2. Qxe6 +, followed by taking the Bishop then on d6, gives White a winning advantage.

Another defensive effort would be 1 . . . Nd8, protecting both pawns rather than seizing White's Knight. The problem here is that 2. Rac1 drives the Queen to unfavorable spots. If 2 . . . Qa5, then 3. Nxb7 wins a pawn for starters. If instead 2 . . . Qd7, then 3. Nb5 Qe8 4. Nc7 takes a Rook. And no better is 2 . . . Qb8, which is annihilated by 3. Rc8. **White Wins.**
1–0 (50)

WHITE: **Karpov**   TACTIC: **PASSED PAWN**
BLACK: **Kasparov**
WHERE: **Moscow 1985, Match Game 2**
POSSIBLE POSITION

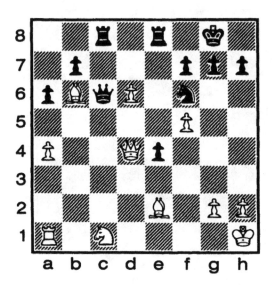

BLACK TO MOVE

ANALYSIS: The Queen protects the Bishop and the Rook, which protects the Knight, which protects the Bishop, which guards the back rank. With all that, there's no defense to **1 . . . Qxc1+!**, when **2. Rxc1 Rxc1+ 3. Bd1 e3** (the race begins) **4. d7 e2 5. dxe8/Q+ Nxe8** and Black's promoting pawn surges on. **Black Wins.**
Draw (65)

WHITE: Karpov   TACTIC: DEFLECTION
BLACK: Kasparov
WHERE: Moscow 1985, Match Game 2
POSSIBLE POSITION

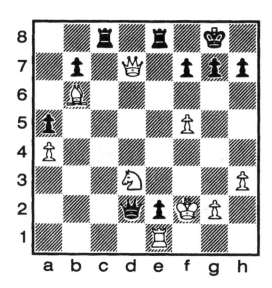

BLACK TO MOVE

ANALYSIS: The White Bishop is a pillar of strength over two vital points: d8 and e3. If Black could move a Rook safely to d8 he would hook the Knight, and if his Queen could safely move to e3, he could mate. The Bishop can't do double duty. So Black plays **1 ... Rcd8!**, when White must move his Queen away, surrendering his Knight. **Black Wins.**
Draw (65)

WHITE: **Karpov**   TACTIC: **REMOVING THE GUARD**
BLACK: **Kasparov**
WHERE: **Moscow 1985, Match Game 2**
POSSIBLE POSITION

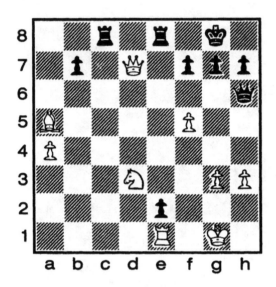

BLACK TO MOVE

ANALYSIS: On 1 . . . Qxh3, White might be able to put over 2. Rxe2, when 2 . . . Rxe2 permits 3. Qxc8+. This line loses water, however, after the penetrating **1 . . . Qe3+**. After **2. Kg2** (not 2. Nf2 because of 2 . . . Qxg3+) **2 . . . b6 3. Bb4**, Black expropriates the Knight by 3 . . . Rcd8. **Black Wins.**
Draw (65)

WHITE: **Karpov**   TACTIC: **PIN**
BLACK: **Kasparov**
WHERE: **Moscow 1985, Match Game 4**
POSSIBLE POSITION

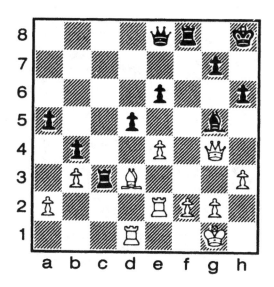

BLACK TO MOVE

ANALYSIS: White's ill-placed pieces are stepping on each other. Black's Rooks—one anchored at c3 and the other patrolling the f-file—and dominant Bishop command the greater half of the board. It all cashes in with **1 . . . Rf4**. White has to shift back to the third rank with **2. Qg3**, after which **2 . . . dxe4** stomps the pinned Bishop at d3. Black's Rook at c3 prevents the Bishop from moving off the rank, for that would lose the Queen. **Black Wins.**
1–0 (63)

WHITE: **Karpov**   TACTIC: **MATING ATTACK**
BLACK: **Kasparov**
WHERE: **Moscow 1985, Match Game 4**
POSSIBLE POSITION

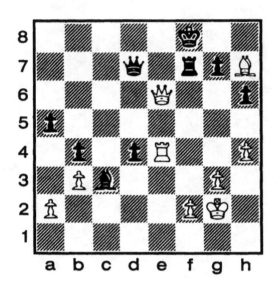

WHITE TO MOVE

ANALYSIS: Black's King can be corralled. The Bishop prevents escape to g8, and the doubled major pieces on the e-file cut 'em off at the pass. The coup de grâce is **1. Qe5!**. The threat is then 2. Qb8 followed by capturing Black's Queen off the back rank with mate. Three piddling primary defensive tries:

A) If 1 . . . Rf6, to create an escape hatch, then 2. Qb8+ Kf7 3. Qg8 is mate.

B) If 1 . . . Re7, then 2. Qf4+ Ke8 (2 . . . Rf7 walks right into 3. Qb8+) 3. Bg6+ Kd8 4. Qb8+ (or 4. Qf8+) wins at least a Rook.

C) If 1 . . . Qd8, then 2. Qc5+ Re7 3. Rf4+ Ke8 4. Qc6+ Qd7 (4 . . . Rd7 5. Bg6+ or 5. Qg6+ Ke7 6. Rf7+ Ke8 7. Rf6+ Ke7 8. Qf7 mate) 5. Bg6+ Kd8 6. Rf8+ is curtains. **White Wins.**
1–0 (63)

WHITE: Karpov   TACTIC: **BALANCE**
BLACK: Kasparov
WHERE: Moscow 1985, Match Game 10
ACTUAL POSITION

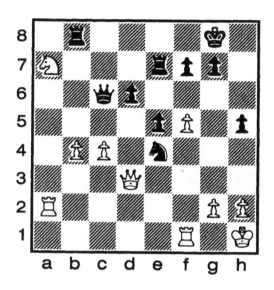

BLACK TO MOVE

White might set up a powerful consolidation on the Queenside by b5 and Nc6 unless stopped. Thus, Kasparov sacked the exchange, **1 . . . Rxa7 2. Rxa7**, and continued **2 . . . Rxb4**, to expunge the dangerous Knight and b-pawn. Since White had to give up on his c-pawn, he switched to counterattack with **3. Qf3**, aimed at the h-pawn. After **3 . . . Rxc4 4. Qxh5 Nf2 +!**, draw was written on the wall. Play went **5. Kg1** (5. Rxf2 Rc1 +) **5 . . . Nh3 +!**, and if 6. Qxh3 (or 6. gxh3) then 6 . . . Qc5 + swipes the Rook at a7. After **6. Kh1 Nf2 + 7. Kg1**, the players agreed to a **Draw**.
Draw (37)

WHITE: **Kasparov**   TACTIC: **DISCOVERED ATTACK**
BLACK: **Karpov**
WHERE: **Moscow 1985, Match Game 11**
ACTUAL POSITION

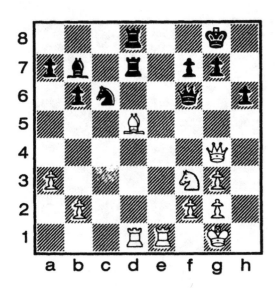

WHITE TO MOVE

ANALYSIS: One of the truly star-bright moments of the great match. Karpov routinely had doubled Rooks on the d-file in symbiotic protection. This partnership was immediately dissolved with the shocking **1. Qxd7!!**. After the compulsory **1 . . . Rxd7 2. Re8+ Kh7 3. Be4+, Black Resigned**. On 3 . . . g6 4. Rxd7 Ba6 5. Bxc6, White has two Rooks and a Knight for the Queen. Of course, 5 . . . Qxc6 can't make it because of 6. Rxf7 mate.
1–0 (25)

WHITE: **Karpov**   TACTIC: **KINGSIDE ATTACK**
BLACK: **Kasparov**
WHERE: **Moscow 1985, Match Game 16**
ACTUAL POSITION

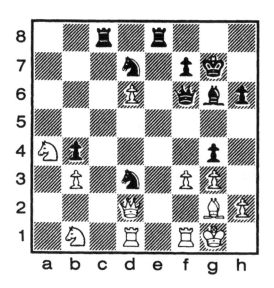

BLACK TO MOVE

ANALYSIS: Karpov's last move (f3) was a bid for freedom, for, despite his edge in pawns, his pieces are suffocating. The intrusive Black Knight at d3 hinders the heavy pieces (note, neither Rook can safely move). White's own Knights lack purpose and are about to fall off the board. Kasparov pushed Karpov into the night of the living dead with **1 . . . Qxd6**. This meanwhile freed the Knight at d7, where it was blockading the d-pawn.

White clung to his material with **2. fxg4**, but he might have erroneously attempted 2. Nb2, to energize his pieces. That would fail to 2 . . . Qd4 + 3. Kh1 Qxb2 4. Qxb2 Nxb2 5. Rxd7 Bd3 6. Rg1 Rc2 7. fxg4 (what else?) 7 . . . Ree2 8. Rd4 (to stop . . . Be4) 8 . . . Bb5 9. Rd6 (otherwise . . . Bc6) 9 . . . Nd3 10. h3 Nf2 + 11. Kh2

Ne4 12. Rb6 Ng5 13. Rxb5 Nf3+ 14. Kh1 Rxg2 15. Rxg2 Rc1+ 16. Rg1 Rxg1 mate.

After **2. fxg4**, the game continued **2 . . . Qd4+ 3. Kh1 Nf6 4. Rf4 Ne4 5. Qxd3**. With two minutes left on his clock to make six moves, coup-de-maître Karpov is at a loss to defend himself from **5 . . . Nf2+ 6. Rxf2** (6. Kg1 Nh3++ 7. Kh1 Qxd3 8. Rxd3 Re1+ wins the house) **6 . . . Bxd3 7. Rfd2 Qe3 8. Rxd3**.

It would appear that White still had material equality, for he possessed two Knights and a Bishop for the Queen. They didn't help in this position, as the demon Kasparov readily demonstrated:

9 . . . Rc1 10. Nb2 (10. Rxe3 Rxd1+ followed by 11 . . . Rxe3, and White loses his shirt) **10 . . . Qf2 11. Nd2** (on 11. Rxc1 Re1+ mates in three moves) **11 . . . Rxd1+** (or 11 . . . Re2 kills too) **12. Nxd1 Re1+**, and again Black mates in three. However White blocks on f1, Black takes first with his Rook and second with his Queen. **White Resigned.**

0–1 (40)

WHITE: **Kasparov**   TACTIC: **DOUBLE ATTACK**
BLACK: **Karpov**
WHERE: **Moscow 1985, Match Game 17**
POSSIBLE POSITION

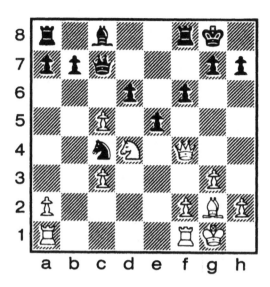

WHITE TO MOVE

ANALYSIS: White's Knight and Queen are pawn-forked, but it's not so simple. The question is, who's losing the piece? After **1. Bd5+ Kh8 2. Nb5**, it appears Black is, for his Knight at c4 has no future. If Black moves his Queen, White's Queen takes the Knight; and if Black takes White's Queen first, then White takes Black's Queen, leaving Black two attacked pieces, the Rook at a8 and the hapless c4-Knight. **White Wins.**
Draw (29)

WHITE: **Kasparov**   TACTIC: **PIN**
BLACK: **Miles**
WHERE: **Basel 1986, Match Game 1**
ACTUAL POSITION

WHITE TO MOVE

ANALYSIS: White should obliterate Black's Rook with 1. Nxb7, though after 1 . . . e3+ 2. Ka2 Bxg6 3. fxe3 (or 3. Rxg6 exf2 threatening to make a new Queen) 3 . . . Qe4, Black has some slight chances to complicate the game. Kasparov tried to clarify the position with **1. Rf6?!,** but that should lead to a draw by 1 . . . e3+! 2. Nxf5 exf2! 3. Rxg7+ Rhxg7 4. Ne7+ Rbxe7 5. Rxf4 Re1+ 6. Ka2 f1 (Q) 7. Rxf1 Rxf1, when Black's two Rooks can generate formidable threats of their own. Instead, Miles blundered on the final move of the time control with **1 . . . Qh2?,** and lost after **2. Rg3 Qh1+ 3. Ka2,** when **Black Resigned.** He can't defend against the double threat to his Bishop at f5 and Rook at b7.
1–0 (42)

WHITE: **Miles**   TACTIC: **FORK AND PIN**
BLACK: **Kasparov**
WHERE: **Basel 1986, Match Game 6**
ACTUAL POSITION

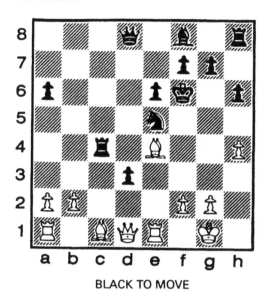

BLACK TO MOVE

ANALYSIS: In this woolly-wild position, Black's King looks exposed, but more important is his greater centralization and horrific passed pawn. Kasparov wins by **1 . . . Rxc1!**. Now if 2. Qxc1, then 2 . . . d2 will swamp the Rook at e1 with check and put Black a piece ahead. The game went on: **2. Rxc1 d2 3. Rf1 Qd4**, threatening the Bishop. If 4. Bb1, then 4 . . . dxc1 (Q) 5. Qxd4 Qc7 endows Black with a fine game. And if White then tries to exploit the frozen Knight at e5 by 6. f4, then 6 . . . Bc5 pins White's Queen.

So White answered 3 . . . Qd4 with **4. Rc2**, and the game rolled along: **4 . . . Qxe4 5. Rxd2 Bc5 6. Re1 Qxh4 7. Qc2** (on 6. a3 Black lurks with the troublesome 6 . . . Ng4, attacking f2 and supporting invasion at h2) **7 . . . Bb4 8. Rxe5 Bxd2 9. g3 Qd4 10. Re4 Qd6**, and **White Resigned.** Miles has no compensation for being down a Bishop.
0–1 (29)

WHITE: **Karpov**   TACTIC: **COUNTERATTACK**
BLACK: **Kasparov**
WHERE: **London 1986, Match Game 1**
ACTUAL POSITION

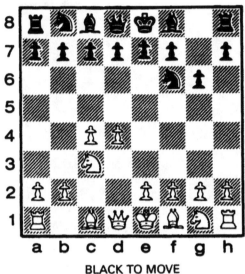

BLACK TO MOVE

ANALYSIS: The first game of a championship match can set the tone for an entire match. Are the combatants tentative or decisive? Should the champion wait for the challenger to falter or should he strike out for the initiative? Kasparov left no doubt of his aggressive intentions when he advanced **3 . . . d5,** signifying the Gruenfeld Defense. This often risky counter is seldom seen in championship games, and for Kasparov it represents a radical departure from his favorite King's Indian Defense, 3 . . . Bg7. Karpov must have been surprised. Rather than engage a sharp fight with 4.cxd5, Karpov chose the stolid **4.Nf3** to avoid complications. In this first game of his first title defense, Kasparov demonstrates his gladiatorial spirit.
Draw (21)

THE KASPAROV TEST

Most everyone tries to beat the best, which means top competitors get precious little respite. With nothing to lose, the underdog has a supreme psychological advantage. He can breezily set insidious traps that may work—even against someone like Gary Kasparov. A champ must be constantly on guard to ward off surprises that may topple him.

The following ten examples show pitfalls that Kasparov might have fallen into, or, in one case, a snare he actually did succumb to. Each example is preceded by a question. You will be asked to find the best move, or choose between two moves, or, in one instance, to determine if a certain move wins.

Examine the diagram and try to answer the question. Then compare your answer with the analysis of the position. Give yourself one point for every correct answer and zero if you get it wrong. Total your correct answers and grade yourself according to the accompanying chart.

Kasparov Test Chart

EXCELLENT	9-10	right
VERY GOOD	7-8	right
GOOD	5-6	right
AVERAGE	3-4	right
YOU NEED MORE WORK	1-2	right
CHECKERS ANYONE?	0	right

WHITE: **Karpov**   TACTIC: **DISCOVERED CHECK**
BLACK: **Kasparov**
WHERE: **Moscow 1984-85, Match Game 41**
POSSIBLE POSITION
What is White's best move?

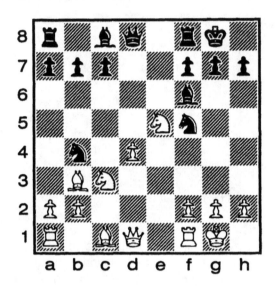

WHITE TO MOVE

ANALYSIS: Black exerts pressure against the d-pawn, but White's offensive against f7 is more biting, beginning with **1. Nxf7!**. Black can choose from two main defenses:

A) He can kaput the Knight with his Rook, 1 . . . Rxf7. That bottoms out after 2. Bxf7+ Kxf7 3. Qb3+, winning back the Knight on b4 and leaving White up the exchange.

B) He can nail down White's d-pawn, 1 . . . Qxd4. That disappoints after 2. Qh5! Qh4 (trying to force a trade of Queens) 3. Ne5+ Kh8 4. Ng6 mate, for the h-pawn is pinned. **White Wins.** Draw (71)

WHITE: Belyavsky   TACTIC: **IN-BETWEEN CHECK**
BLACK: Kasparov
WHERE: Moscow 1983

POSSIBLE POSITION
Should White play 1. Nxc6 or 1. Qg4 + ?

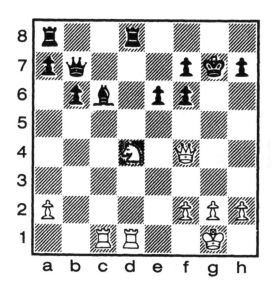

WHITE TO MOVE

ANALYSIS: Black has two extra pawns, though his Bishop is assaulted twice and guarded once. Yet 1. Nxc6 doesn't work because of 1 . . . Rxd1 + (diverting away the defense of c6) 2. Rxd1 Qxc6. But White attempts **1. Qg4 + !** first. This covers d1, so that after **1 . . . Kf8 2. Nxc6 Rxd1 +**, White holds with **3. Qxd1. White Wins.**
1–0 (38)

WHITE: **Korchnoi**   TACTIC: **MATING NET**
BLACK: **Kasparov**
WHERE: **Lucerne 1982**

POSSIBLE POSITION

What is White's best move?

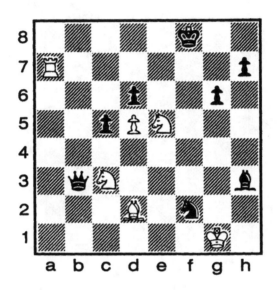

WHITE TO MOVE

ANALYSIS: White wins by **1. Bh6+ Ke8 2. Ra8+ Ke7 3. Bg5 mate.** Nothing else is as strong as this. **White Wins.**
0–1 (36)

WHITE: Razuvaev   TACTIC: **MATING ATTACK**
BLACK: Kasparov
WHERE: USSR 1978
POSSIBLE POSITION
What is White's best move?

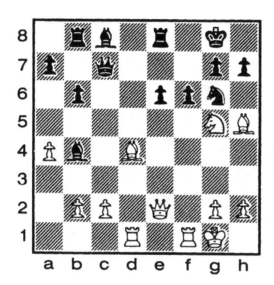

WHITE TO MOVE

ANALYSIS: Black is now shielded, but only briefly. The game goes on: **1. Nxh7! Kxh7 2. Bxg6+ Kxg6 3. Qg4+ Kf7 4. Qh5+ Kf8** (5 . . . Ke7 6. Bxf6+!) **5. Rxf6+!** (White is hellbent on a breakthrough sacrifice) **5 . . . gxf6 6. Qh8+ 6 . . . Kf7** (or 6 . . . Ke7 7. Bxf6+ Kf7 8. Qg7 mate) **7. Qxf6+ Kg8 8. Qh8+ Kf7 9. Qg7 mate. White Wins.**
1–0 (35)

WHITE: **Kasparov**   TACTIC: **THE VULNERABLE**
BLACK: **Karpov**   **BACK RANK**
WHERE: **Moscow 1984-85, Match Game 6**
POSSIBLE POSITION
Does White win by 1. Ne7 + ?

WHITE TO MOVE

ANALYSIS: Can White play **1. Ne7 +** here? Surely! The main variation goes 1. Ne7 + Bxe7 2. Rxe7 Rc1 + 3. Bf1 Kf8 4. Rxa7 Bc8 5. Bb2 Rb1 6. Rxa2 Bh3 7. Ra1, which is stocked with everything and wins.

This line was crafted by former world champion Boris Spassky and U.S. champion Lev Alburt at the Manhattan Chess Club. Spassky just happened to drop in at the end of Alburt's lecture.

The bitter truth, however, is that **1. Ne7 +** does not win. According to world-class challenger Artur Yusupov, in a very fine piece of analysis, the problem develops after **1 . . . Bxe7 2. Rxe7**. Here Black shouldn't continue with 2 . . . Rc1 +, for that leads to loss. Black can save the day, however, by **2 . . . b4!**, when **3. h4 Nc3 4. d6 Bb5 5. Rxa7 Rd8! 6. Rb7 Be8 7. Rxb4 Nb5 8. Be5 f6! 9. Bd5 + Kf8 10. Bb2 Rxd6** gives Black an equal game.
0–1 (70)

WHITE: **Belyavsky**   TACTIC: **DOUBLE ATTACK**
BLACK: **Kasparov**   **(PAWN FORK)**
WHERE: **Moscow 1983, Match Game 4**
ACTUAL POSITION
Should White play 1. Nf5 + or 1. f4?

WHITE TO MOVE

ANALYSIS: In this perplexing but materially equivalent situation, Gary Kasparov actually blundered, throwing away the game he had gallantly managed to hold so far. With **1. Nf5 +** (not 1. f4 Qxh4) **1 . . . Kg6** (to threaten the capture of the Knight by 2 . . . Qxf5) **2. Ne7+ + Kh6 3. f4,** Black had nothing better than submission, a decision he exercised. **Black Resigned.**
1–0 (38)

WHITE: **Alburt**　　　　TACTIC: **DOUBLE ATTACK-FORK**
BLACK: **Kasparov**
WHERE: **Lucerne 1982**
POSSIBLE POSITION
What is White's best move?

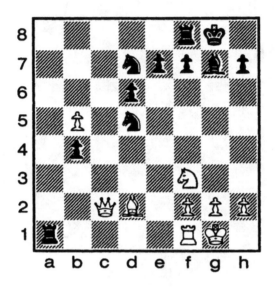

WHITE TO MOVE

ANALYSIS: Here Kasparov has a Rook, Knight, and two pawns for the Queen, but the loose nature of the position favors her ladyship, for the Queen is able to attack in multiple directions. Gary parts company with one of his pieces after **1. Rxa1 Bxa1 2. Qa2**, forking the Bishop and Knight at d5. **White Wins.**
0–1 (57)

WHITE: **Kasparov**   TACTIC: **DESPERADO**
BLACK: **Pribly**
WHERE: **Skara 1980**
ACTUAL POSITION
Should White play 1. Qxc5 or 1. Rd6?

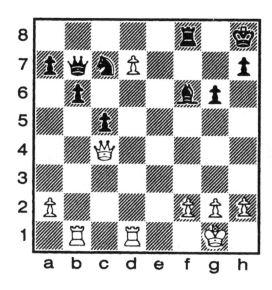

WHITE TO MOVE

ANALYSIS: Black has a Bishop and Knight for a Rook, but White's potent passed pawn requires crystal-clear attention. White can try to pick up a pawn with 1. Qxc5 because of the pin on the b-pawn, but Black redeems himself with 1 . . . Qxg2 + ! (a last-ditch tactic, where you grab what you can for a doomed piece). For example, after 2. Kxg2 bxc5 3. Rb7 Ne6 4. Rd6 Nf4 + 5. Kf1 Bd8 6. Rxa7, White gains only a small advantage. Probable Draw.

   In the actual game, Kasparov played the commanding **1. Rd6**, which kept Black's Knight from e6. This is the better move. 1–0 (32)

WHITE: **Kasparov**   TACTIC: **DISCOVERED ATTACK**
BLACK: **Belyavsky**
WHERE: **Moscow 1983, Match Game 5**

POSSIBLE POSITION
Can Black force a win?

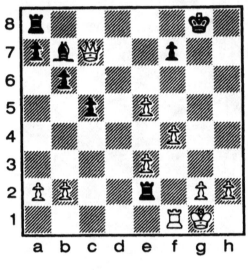

BLACK TO MOVE

ANALYSIS: After the obvious **1 . . . Rxg2 + 2. Kh1,** Black has the potential for a resounding discovered check along the b7-h1 diagonal, but wherever the Rook at g2 moves, White will seize the pesky Bishop. The blast-off is **2 . . . Be4!,** where White has no real way to disturb the Bishop, it being encased by White pawns. If 3. h3, to stop 3 . . . Rg3 discovered mate, then Black actually has the time for 3 . . . Kh8, with the idea of 4 . . . Rag8 and shortly mating or winning material. Sample variations are: A) 4.Qxf7 Rg7 + , winning the Queen; B) 4.e6 (threatening 5.Qe5 +)4 . . . f6 (threatening 5 . . . Rg7 +)5.e7 Rag8 (threatening 6 . . . Rg1 + 7.Kh2 R(8)g2 mate) 6.e8(Q) Rxe8 and Black still has two powerful threats: to double Rooks on the g-file or to give a discovered check, winning White's Queen. **Black Wins.** Kasparov dispassionately avoided this pitfall.

WHITE: **Kasparov**
BLACK: **Tal**
WHERE: **USSR 1983**
POSSIBLE POSITION
What is Black's best move?

TACTIC: **MATING ATTACK**

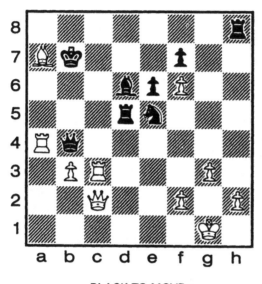

BLACK TO MOVE

ANALYSIS: In this complicated position, White's Rook must not leave the first rank unguarded. Black can exploit this weakening by **1 . . . Nf3 + !**, when **2. Rxf3** (2. Kg2 Ne1 + forks King and Queen) **2 . . . Qe1 + 3. Kg2 Rxh2 + ! 4. Kxh2 Rh5 + 5. Rh4 Rxh4 + 6. Kg2 Qh1** is mate. **Black Wins.**
Draw (43)

GLOSSARY OF TACTICS

Balance Refers to a position in which asymmetrical elements and disparate forces clash to achieve an even, dynamically balanced game, with equal winning chances for both sides.

Centralization Transfer of pieces toward the center before commencing a specific action or plan.

Corridor Mate A mate by a Queen or Rook along an outer rank or file.

Counterattack Defending by diverting your opponent with an attack of your own.

Deflection An attack that lures a hostile piece either to a certain square or away from one.

Desperado Sacrifice of a doomed piece in a way that costs as much as possible to the opponent.

Discovered Attack An attack that occurs when one piece moves out of the way of another piece, thereby unveiling a threat.

Discovered Check A discovered attack to the enemy King.

Double Attack Any attack that threatens the enemy in at least two ways.

Double Check A discovered attack in which both the moving and stationary attackers give check.

Fork A double attack in which a friendly piece threatens to capture at least two unprotected enemy pieces at the same time.

Hand-to-hand Fighting General attack in which both sides exchange constant and varied threats in the same region or for the same goal.

In-between Check An unexpected check played before completing an anticipated sequence of moves already begun (also called *zwischenzug*).

In-between Move An unexpected move played before completing an anticipated sequence of moves already begun (also called *zwischenzug*).

Kingside Attack A general campaign against a castled Kingside position, involving a complexity of threats and maneuvers to bring about a checkmate.

Knight Fork A fork in which a Knight threatens to capture two enemy pieces on the same turn.

Mating Attack An attack usually involving several pieces and pawns leading to a probable checkmate.

Mating Net A direct sequence of moves leading to a forced checkmate.

Outside Passed Pawn A passed pawn removed from the main theater that can be used as a decoy to divert enemy forces in the endgame, especially the opposing King.

Overload A tactic exploiting an enemy piece or pawn's inability to defend in sequence two different points it's already guarding.

Passed Pawn A pawn that has moved beyond the other side's pawns, and is thus freed to move toward promotion. No enemy pawn can stop it.

Pawn Fork A threat by a pawn to capture either of two enemy pieces on the same turn.

Penetration An endgame concept whereby an invading King, in conjunction with supporting forces, can work its way into the enemy's position, overcoming or piercing a defensive barrier or wall.

Perpetual Check A set of checks that do not lead to mate but repeat the position and force a draw.

Pin An attack that prevents or dissuades an enemy unit from moving off a particular line for fear of exposing another unit or important square to capture. The pinned unit shields a more valuable piece and thus is vulnerable to further threats.

Removing the Guard Undermining a piece's protection by capturing the defender or forcing it to move away.

Skewer A double attack in which one piece attacks two enemy pieces along the same line, usually compelling the first piece to move, exposing the second to capture. The opposite of a pin, it requires the more valuable enemy unit to be in front of a lesser compatriot.

Smothered Mate A checkmate by a Knight in which the losing King's escape squares are all blocked by its own forces.

Trap A disguised threat designed to lull an unsuspecting opponent into an error.

Trapped Piece An attacked piece that has no escape and will be lost.

Triangulation A tactic in the endgame whereby a King maneuvers to recreate its current position while transferring the turn to play to his opponent. The same position thus results but with the other side to move.

Vulnerable Back Rank Implementing actions the enemy can't defend against for fear of being checkmated on the back rank.

Winning the Exchange Gaining a Rook for a Bishop or Knight.

Zugzwang A situation in which any move you make worsens your position.

TOURNAMENT AND MATCH RESULTS

Date	Event	+	–	=	Place
1976					
January	USSR Junior Championship, Tbilisi	5	0	4	1
1977					
January	USSR Junior Championship, Riga	8	0	1	1
1978					
January	Sokolsky Memorial Tournament, Minsk	11	2	4	1
June-July	USSR Championship Elimination Tournament, Daugavpils	6	1	6	1
December	46th USSR Championship (Premier League), Tbilisi	4	4	9	9
1979					
April	International Tournament, Banja Luka	8	0	7	1
July	USSR Spartakiad, Moscow (board 2)	4	1	3	2
December	47th USSR Championship (Premier League), Minsk	6	3	8	3-4
1980					
January	European Team Championship, Skara (board 10)	5	0	1	1
April	USSR Central Chess Club international tournament, Baku	8	0	7	1
August	World Junior Championship, Dortmund	8	0	5	1
November-December	24th World Olympiad, Malta (board 6)	8	1	3	2

Date	Event	+	–	=	Place
1981					
February	Match-Tournament of USSR Teams, Moscow (board 1)	3	1	2	1
April	Grandmaster Tournament, Moscow	3	1	9	2-4
May	USSR Team Championship (1st League), Moscow (board 1)	4	0	5	1
August	World Junior Team Championship, Graz (board 1)	8	0	2	1
October	Grandmaster tournament, Tilburg	3	3	5	6-8
December	49th USSR Championship (Premier League), Frunze	10	2	5	1-2
1982					
May	Grandmaster tournament, Bugojno	6	0	7	1
September	Interzonal tournament, Moscow	7	0	6	1
November-December	25th World Olympiad, Lucerne (board 2)	6	0	5	1
1983					
February-March	Candidates Quarter-final Match v. Belyavsky, Moscow	4	1	4	
August-September	Grandmaster tournament, Niksic	9	1	4	1
November-December	Candidates Semi-final Match v. Korchnoi, London	4	1	6	
1984					
March-April	Candidates Final Match v. Smyslov, Vilnius	4	0	9	
June	USSR-Rest of the World (v. Timman) (board 2)	1	0	3	
September-February	World Championship Match v. Karpov, Moscow	3	5	40	
1985					
May-June	Match v. Hübner, Hamburg	3	0	3	
June	Match v. Andersson, Belgrade	2	0	4	
September-November	World Championship Match v. Karpov, Moscow	5	3	16	
December	Match v. Timman, Hilversum	3	1	2	
1986					
May	Match v. Miles, Basel	5	0	1	

INDEX OF TACTICS

About the Author

Bruce Pandolfini, a U.S. National Chess Master, gained prominence as an analyst on PBS's live telecast of the Fischer-Spassky championship match in 1972. In due course, he lectured widely on chess and in 1978 was chosen to deliver the Bobby Fischer Chess Lectures at the University of Alabama in Birmingham. His first book, *Let's Play Chess,* appeared in 1980. The author is a *Chess Life* magazine consulting editor, for which he writes the monthly "ABCs of Chess." He is the author of *Bobby Fischer's Outrageous Chess Moves, One-Move Chess by the Champions, Principles of the New Chess* and *The ABCs of Chess,* and has also written columns for *Time-Video,* the *Litchfield County Times,* and *Physician's Travel and Meeting Guide.*

As a chess teacher, he's been on the faculty of the New School for Social Research since 1973, and currently conducts chess classes at Browning, Trinity, and the Little Red School House in New York City. With U.S. Champion Lev Alburt, he has developed special children's programs sponsored by the American Chess Foundation. The director of the world famous Manhattan Chess Club at Carnegie Hall, Pandolfini visited the USSR in the fall of 1984 to study Russian teaching methods and observe the controversial championship match between Anatoly Karpov and Gary Kasparov.

FIRESIDE CHESS LIBRARY

**Just a reminder about the treasure of chess books from Fireside,
for all players from beginners to advanced chess masters!**

NEW TITLES:

RUSSIAN CHESS
Bruce Pandolfini
144 pgs, 61984-5, $6.95

**KASPAROV'S WINNING CHESS
TACTICS**
Bruce Pandolfini
208 pgs, 61985-3, $6.95

ABC'S OF CHESS
Bruce Pandolfini
128 pgs, 61982-9, $6.95

LET'S PLAY CHESS
Bruce Pandolfini
192 pgs, 61983-7, $6.95

CHESS BACKLIST:

CHESS FOR BEGINNERS
I.A. Horowitz
134 pgs, 21184-6, $5.95

CHESS OPENINGS
I.A. Horowitz
792 pgs, 20553-6, $16.95

CHESS TRAPS
I.A. Horowitz & Fred Reinfeld
250 pgs, 21041-6, $6.95

HOW TO THINK AHEAD IN CHESS
I.A. Horowitz & Fred Reinfeld
274 pgs, 21138-2, $6.95

THE CHESS COMPANION
Irving Chernev
288 pgs, 21651-1, $9.95

CHESS THE EASY WAY
Reuben Fine
186 pgs, 0-346-12323-2, $5.95

**THE MOST INSTRUCTIVE GAMES
OF CHESS EVER PLAYED**
Irving Chernev
286 pgs, 21536-1, $8.95

PRINCIPLES OF THE NEW CHESS
Bruce Pandolfini
144 pgs, 60719-7, $6.95 (Available
March '86)

AN INVITATION TO CHESS
Irving Chernev & Kenneth Harkness
224 pgs, 21270-2, $5.95

LOGICAL CHESS, MOVE BY MOVE
Irving Chernev
250 pgs, 21135-8, $7.95

WINNING CHESS
Irving Chernev & Fred Reinfeld
236 pgs, 21114-5, $7.95

**HOW TO WIN IN THE CHESS
OPENINGS**
I.A. Horowitz
192 pgs, 0-346-12445-X, $5.95

**BOBBY FISCHER'S OUTRAGEOUS
CHESS MOVES**
Bruce Pandolfini
128 pgs, 60609-3, $6.95

**THE 1,000 BEST SHORT GAMES
OF CHESS**
Irving Chernev
562 pgs, 53801-2, $7.95

THE FIRESIDE BOOK OF CHESS
Irving Chernev & Fred Reinfeld
406 pgs, 21221-4, $8.95

**ONE MOVE CHESS BY THE
CHAMPIONS**
Bruce Pandolfini
128 pgs, 60608-5, $6.95